Ascend to JOY

TRANSFORM YOUR LIFE THROUGH LIVING KABBALAH

D0809172

Ascend to JOY

TRANSFORM YOUR LIFE THROUGH LIVING KABBALAH

CHRISTINE ELWART

O'LEARY PUBLISHING
The Influencer's Press

BONITA SPRINGS, FL

Copyright © 2020 by Christine Elwart

All rights reserved.

Published in the United States by
O'Leary Publishing
www.olearypublishing.com

The views, information, or opinions expressed in this book are solely those of the authors involved and do not necessarily represent those of O'Leary Publishing, LLC.

ISBN: 978-1-7341589-8-4 (print)
ISBN: 978-1-7341589-9-1 (ebook)
Library of Congress Control Number: 2020905963

Photography by Louis Venne Photography
Editing by Heather Davis Desrocher
Line Editing by Mathew Acton
Proofreading by Sharman Monro
Cover and interior design by Jessica Angerstein

Printed in the United States of America

This book is dedicated to:

The Seekers in this World

CONTENTS

PREFACE

Pathway of Discovery

In the Universal Kabbalah, we focus on having fun with ourselves, with the entity that we are and finding true joy in the answers to our questions.

—GUDNI GUDNASON

Are you ready to experience more joy than you ever thought possible?

You must be because you picked up this book as part of your journey. In this book, I will share with you a method of discovery that has been used for thousands of years by some of the wisest, most powerful and successful people in history. People like Carl Jung, Nicola Tesla, Michelangelo and Da Vinci, to name a few who used this method.

This method of discovery, called Kabbalah, contains a map to the remarkable truth of who you are and the possibility of who you can become, which is literally in your DNA. Kabbalah is the road map back to GOD and to our true selves. This book offers you the chance to step out of the confines of life, as you have known it. My goal is to open the door to limitless possibilities for you by sharing my story with the conviction that it can be your story as well.

What you are experiencing now is only one possibility of life. The process described in these pages can guide you to a more authentic version of yourself and your life. What if there have been hidden signs throughout your experience here on earth? What if you could learn to not only read those signs, but also determine the path that will lead you to joy?

My life journey has been filled with signs. The sign that led me to writing this book had an arrow pointing to a path that was unfamiliar and hidden by brush that parted only when I took the next step. Have you ever had that experience? A path opens up, and you cannot see exactly where it is leading. Pretty much everyday life, right? Well, let me introduce you to a way of discovering how to interpret the signs so that you can step into your destiny.

Are you moving? Or are you stuck?

At the time of this writing, I am sixty-eight years old. I've been married for forty-six years, raised four daughters, nurtured my grandchildren and grown numerous communities. It has been both challenging and fulfilling, and I always want to keep growing and moving. But at this point, most people would expect me to be ready for retirement. And yet, here I am writing a book.

I will say that I never intended to write a book. Seriously. And then, through a series of incredible circumstances, powered by the Kabbalah process of discovery, I got a very clear, very distinct message from God to do just that. Write a book - this book. And so, I took the next step on that path hidden by brush.

This is not a scholarly book. It is meant to be inspirational and to introduce you to Universal Kabbalah. It is my experience and, thus, is life as seen through a single lens, a lens that is looking for the Light. I offer it to you as an insight into what life can be and what it has come to mean for one woman, me.

Kabbalah is not a doctrine - you do not need to believe anything. It is a system of discovering truth through direct experience. Interested? Then hop in the car and get ready to create the life of your dreams.

As my photographer, Louis Venne, said today, "Photography is about looking for the light, the right light." Well this book is about Light as well. He also said, "There are three types of people in this world - those leading the parade, those following the leaders and those who do not know there is a parade." Let this book be your sign and come join the parade, if you haven't already.

Some of you have always known that there is something more. For you, it will be a matter of remembering what you have innately known. For others, it may awaken in you the promise that has been nestled in the recesses of your DNA. Wherever you are in the parade, welcome to the life of incredible possibilities that breaks through the glass ceiling of your limiting beliefs.

My hope is that you will read and experience this book and have new hope - hope that there is something working deeply within you that is all about living life fully because you are more than you can imagine and your life matters.

Take note of the date you started reading this book. Write it down. You can look back at it and know that this was a time of awakening.

Happy Kabbalah!!

INTRODUCTION

The Beginning of Living Kabbalah

There is a difference between a book of two hundred pages from the very beginning and a book of two hundred pages which is the result of an original eight hundred pages. The six hundred are there, only you don't see them.

—ELIE WIESEL

June 2019

To begin, we will start at the end. I am waiting in the airport after my final ascension retreat for Kabbalah. The flight has been delayed for six hours, and I have time to reflect on all the truly miraculous things I experienced and witnessed this weekend. This is my second journey through The Modern Mystery School's Universal Kabbalah ascension experience, and my heart is full of the love and miracles that I was immersed in this weekend. How I arrived at this point is a story to be told later in the book, so stay tuned.

For now, let me explain the word ascension, which is part of the process I experienced, because it is a primary distinction between this Universal Kabbalah and other forums and experiences. However, I warn you that any explanation pales next to the actual experience.

Ascension, as explained by the Modern Mystery School, means to go up. In the Kabbalah manual that we receive at the beginning of this learning experience, it says:

> *We are here talking about the heightening of one's consciousness to a higher level. As a result, we become more aware of ourselves and the world around us.*
>
> *We ascend into a higher dimension of understanding and we have access to much more knowledge as we ascend higher. There are many different ascension processes. Some of these have been kept secret for a long time; while others have been available to us for a long time.*
>
> *The ascension process that we work with in the Kabbalah has been kept secret and was unknown to the general public until 1888. This is when the Golden Dawn translated most of the secret work that had been kept hidden or unattainable.*
>
> *The ascension that we work with has to do with the Tree of Life. As we ascend up the Tree, learning about the Tree and*

its different aspects, we expand our mind and grow in the understanding of life and life's mysteries.

The final ascension weekend in Universal Kabbalah is the culmination of ten to twelve months of learning and experiences designed to dynamically expose and remove those areas in our ego that no longer serve us. And, while doing this, to activate those parts of us that will bring in the energies to manifest the life of our dreams. The ultimate goal is to *receive* all that we need to live from our Higher Self every moment of every day.

Can you imagine? As Kabbalists, we have the opportunity to create the life of our dreams. It is a mystical journey that has been passed down for thousands of years for our spiritual progression. And, because the Modern Mystery School opened to the public in 1997, it is now available to everyone. Yes, it is available to you. We are in a unique period in the history of mankind and the tools in this study of Kabbalah are divinely designed to help us meet the challenge.

Through the journey of Universal Kabbalah, I witnessed both subtle and dramatic shifts not only within myself, but also in others as well. We are being offered the opportunity to bring light into the darkness.

This is for everyone who engages in Kabbalah. You are no exception. If you choose to take this class, this is for you. If you have DNA, and I know you do, then you can be part of this quest as well. Sound intriguing? Well hang on to your seats.

THE TANGIBLE, MEASURABLE RESULTS

Tell me something, and I will listen. But show me something, and I will pay attention. Kabbalah has captured my attention over and over again because of the results people receive during the process. The saying "the proof is in the pudding," means that you can only judge the quality of something after you have tried, used, or experienced it. Well, I can tell you that Kabbalah is delicious.

At the beginning of the Universal Kabbalah ascension journey, we were asked to think of and write down what our ideal life would look like. We were asked, "What do you want to create? What is the life you want to manifest?" From here, we were asked to set some specific goals with Tangible, Measurable Results (TMRs) in writing. My TMR was to transition from my psychological practice of twenty-six years into full-time work as a certified Guide, Teacher and Healer for the Modern Mystery School and as a spiritual life coach. My measure of achievement would be to have fifteen clients a week.

Imagine my surprise when I reached that goal three months early! I remember feeling happy and exultantly declaring, "I achieved my Tangible, Measurable Result!" I couldn't believe how quickly it had happened.

Almost immediately, I heard that quiet voice, which I identify as God, resounding within, saying, "And what about Our Tangible, Measurable Result?" I was stunned by the directness and power of the question. Curiously, I asked,

"What is Your Tangible, Measurable Result?"

The answer was instant and firm. *Write a book.*

Write a book.

You guessed it. This is the book. Not only do I feel guided to write this book, but I have also experienced so much transformational healing during the course of writing this book that I feel an instant welling up of gratitude even as I type these words.

However, my experience is that anything worthwhile is not without challenges. As my Kabbalah teacher, Eric, says, "Growth happens outside of our comfort zone."

Writing this book takes me way beyond my comfort zone, and it may challenge your sensibilities as well. How can someone brought up in the Roman Catholic Church, who spent years in active ministry as a youth minister and chairperson of the religion department in a Catholic high school find God in Kabbalah? How does a leader in a large charismatic Catholic prayer group become open to ancient teachings of a Mystery School that are outside the scope of what is acceptable to many of her friends and family?

It's simple and at times excruciating. I listened, I discerned, and I sorted through that which was Truth for me and that which was not. I looked at the fruit of my explorations and followed the trail of Love, Peace, Joy, Patience, Kindness, Goodness, Faithfulness, Gentleness and Self-Control.

It has been simple, but it has not been easy.

I didn't expect to be understood, but I certainly didn't expect the rejection, judgment and betrayal, which you will read about later in this book. I also didn't expect that, in the midst of all this, after the grief and the pain . . . that there would be Limitless Light, that there would be God. You see, I discovered a new lifestyle using the Kabbalah method that is powered by Spirit and uses my imagination to produce a new reality. I found a sanctuary in which miracles occur and Peace, Love and Joy are my companions.

This is seeing life from the eagle's eye view instead of the worm's eye view. No more victimhood, no more hopelessness, helplessness or despair.

I assure you that it is possible because this is my life today. We are all on this journey back to God together, and there are many, many roads, as I have discovered.

Take the next step and allow yourself to live life fully and deeply! Allow yourself to see a life full of loving relationships, financial stability, personal fulfillment in your work and time to enjoy all these things. Come to know the exhilarating path of Universal Kabbalah. Ride along with me on this journey of transformation. The destination is divine. Seat belts on?

MY FELLOW TRAVELERS

I am so grateful for the extraordinary groups of people on the path with me who helped to co-create each ten-month experience. This particular Kabbalah class (2018-2019) consisted of approximately thirty-five people of many ages, races, nationalities and belief systems. We were led by Eric Thompson, an international Guide from Brazil, and Barbara Segura, my Guide and dear sister who is from Naples, Florida. Eric and Barbara provided an amazing blend of masculine and feminine energy, which flowed throughout our journey in a delightful dance with grace and beauty. I was also honored to share this journey with my youngest daughter, Renéa, who is a powerful, dynamic young woman. She is an initiate, Healer, Teacher and Ritual Master in the lineage of King Salomon and was experiencing Kabbalah for the first time.

Along with Barbara and Eric, these amazing people held space for me, and each other through their non-judgmental, exquisite love. Together, we created a universe that wove diverse individual threads into a tapestry of Good and Beauty. Although I was the oldest one in the group, I felt welcomed and cared for. The energy of this very diverse and multi-generational group of people was amplified by their investment in the mystery of Kabbalah and in together *climbing* the Tree of Life.

To see the magical power of Universal Kabbalah, we will, in the next chapter, peek into the lives of some of the other group members to see the Tangible Measurable Results they achieved through living Kabbalah.

Tools of Transformation

For a fuller experience of this book, please consider using two tools which have helped to change lives: meditation and journaling. The benefits of both are evidence-based and are used in the Universal Kabbalah ascension process. You will have an opportunity to do both, should you choose, during the course of this book. Each chapter will end with a meditation and a writing/drawing exercise.

BENEFITS OF MEDITATION

REDUCES STRESS

As a rule, mental, emotional and physical stress increase levels of the stress hormone, cortisol. Cortisol, and the production of certain chemicals, can: disrupt sleep, promote depression and anxiety, increase blood pressure, cloud our thinking and contribute to feeling tired and worn out. There are numerous studies on one style of meditation called mindfulness that show a reduction in the production of cortisol, and other hormones, and their effects on our physical being.

HELPS TO CONTROL ANXIETY

Less stress usually means less anxiety. Again, there is quite a bit of literature to substantiate this hypothesis.

INCREASES EMOTIONAL HEALTH

Meditation helps to install a PAUSE button before expressing ourselves inappropriately.

IMPROVES SLEEP

The relaxation of the mind and body can result in a deeper, healthier sleep pattern.

RAISES OUR AWARENESS

Many people are walking around asleep. They are unaware of their words and behaviors and the effect they are having on the people around them. Meditation brings us into this present moment, which allows us to be able to respond to life rather than react from our unconscious. We become response-able.

HOW TO MEDITATE

There are many ways to meditate. Sifting through the numerous forms of meditation, there is one that you can do as a beginner called za-zen or *sitting meditation.* For those of you more advanced practitioners, this will be familiar to you.

Follow these steps, and you can't go wrong!

1. Sit in a quiet, peaceful place where you will not be disturbed.
2. Make sure your back is straight and well supported.
3. Put your feet flat on the floor and rest your arms in your lap with your hands in a receptive position.
4. Begin by breathing in through your nose and out through your mouth.
5. Breathe deep into your belly and focus on the breath going in and going out.
6. When your thoughts interrupt you, go back to focusing on your breath.

That's it! Simple, right? Yes, simple but not easy. However, with consistent practice, it gets better and better.

BENEFITS OF JOURNALING

USES THE WHOLE BRAIN

The type of journaling suggested in this book is whole-brain journaling, which uses both the right and left hemispheres of the brain and helps to anchor in thoughts and images received during meditation. This form of journaling utilizes both the written word and drawing.

ANCHORS IN THOUGHTS AND IMAGES

By recording your impressions from the meditation in words or drawings, you solidify and validate the information you received.

ENHANCES SELF-DISCOVERY

Through the physical expression of writing or drawing, we become more aware of who we are in the recesses of our unconscious as we bring it to the conscious mind.

It is a non-judgmental forum not only for expression, but also for self-discovery. You can journal with words or with pictures or a combination of the two. Whatever works for you!

BOOSTS YOUR MOOD

The mere act of bringing into the light aspects of ourselves that we may not have been fully aware of, acts much like a valve on a pressure cooker. This allows us to feel lighter and freer.

HOW TO JOURNAL

Have a pen, a pencil, crayons, colored pencils, or whatever medium you choose close at hand.

When you finish with your meditation, begin writing or drawing right away. Be aware of any negative judgements you may have about your writing or drawing. This is for you and no one else. It is you learning about you.

Write or draw until there is a sense of completion. Let it flow.

Look for opportunities to both meditate and journal in this book. Have fun with it!

CHAPTER 1

The Birthing of Tangible, Measurable Results

The most wonderful thing about miracles is that they sometimes happen.

—G.K. CHESTERTON

Julie walked into class, confused about her career and the direction of her life. Robin was depressed, and Fran was anxious. During the ten months of Kabbalah, they each transformed and found the results they had been looking for. Is this a miracle? Is it magic? Or is Kabbalah a very practical set of tools that any human being can use to solve life's most difficult problems?

Kabbalah students in the Modern Mystery School tradition are encouraged to develop and write down their dreams and aspirations as Tangible, Measurable Results (TMRs), and there is a considerable amount of time spent, and some creative processes used, developing these TMRs. I've come to appreciate the wisdom of these exercises because they focus our energy and intentions on specific, positive changes, and they illuminate the ways that the internal parts of this process are working.

It is quite fascinating and exciting to experience the unfolding of these goals in tangible ways, not only personally, but also in the lives of others in the group. In the brief ten months of this class, I witnessed people accomplishing as much intrapsychic healing as I have seen in ten years of intense therapy. The amazing part is not only the deep insights people have about themselves, but also the energy they have to move through issues quickly and to truly dispel things that get in the way of moving forward. And I say this having been a psychotherapist for twenty-six years! Some of these TMRs manifest so powerfully that the process looks miraculous. Are you up for a life of miracles?

Let us look at some of the Tangible Measurable Results that my fellow travelers experienced.

MOTHERING

There was a very deep and profound healing that happened to a dear friend of mine in the group. She had set as one of her Tangible, Measurable Results the healing of her concept of *mother*. She was unsure of exactly how this would happen, but opened herself to the realm of limitless possibilities. The Tangible, Measurable Result would be a positive image of the concept of motherhood for herself.

Shortly after setting this desire, she unexpectedly became pregnant for the first time! Talk about bringing up your issues around motherhood! She systematically had every deep, unhealed part of her mother wound brought to the surface through the loving presence of her unborn child. And, with the support of her incredible partner and everyone in the group, she met each challenge with courage.

Having birthed four daughters myself, I watched her pregnancy with curiosity because it was different from my experiences and the pregnancies of people I knew. She was quietly and amazingly unstoppable. I could visibly see the energy of the Universe supporting her in ways that were magical and mystical.

An example of this happened early on when she was having regular episodes of morning sickness. She reported that she was in the shower one day and was very sick. She recalled the power within her to access the "**kingdom of Spirit embodied in her flesh**" (a Truth About the Self from one of the Kabbalah tools) and commanded the nausea to be gone. And it was, with one or two exceptions, for good. This is living Kabbalah in a very tangible way.

She gave birth to Sophia Rose, a beautiful eight-pound, four-ounce little goddess, and healer in her own right, on October 10, 2019. I recently spoke to Sophia Rose's father, who is also a Kabbalist, and he said that he can feel himself being healed in so many ways by simply having her on his chest. The interaction between this young father and his infant daughter is quite touching. Sophia Rose has presented him with opportunities to heal his own childhood, and I am watching his transformation occur right before my eyes. He is a beautiful example of what it means to live Kabbalah.

It is exciting for me to see Sophia Rose's parents explore what fatherhood and motherhood can be. The children coming into the world today are very different from previous generations and need a different approach that takes into account their existence as energetic beings. I am hopeful that the tools gleaned from Kabbalah will guide this new approach and change the face of parenting as we now know it.

SHOCKING SURPRISES

Another example of living Kabbalah was that of a beautiful young man who was experiencing a lot of resistance during our ten-month process. He shared that, in his past, he had committed a number of felonies and that he had served time in jail. Because of the nature and number of his crimes, he had been sentenced to at least ten years of probation without reprieve. Imagine our shock when he brought with him, to our final weekend, a letter stating that his probationary period was finished! He had no reasonable explanation for this reprieve other than his involvement in Kabbalah. Living Kabbalah is full of surprises.

Even more glorious than the ending of his probation was the evolution of this young man as we witnessed the unveiling of his authentic self, and we saw in his face the birthing of the image of God. He emerged from a place of guardedness to a warm, open presence. How does this happen? Mysteriously, magically and majestically. Living Kabbalah is all about responding to the awakening within us of our divine purpose, and acting accordingly. This is the power of the ancient Universal Kabbalah. This is the power of our return to God!

CLARITY

This awakening was evident as I listened to a young woman present her Tangible, Measurable Results. She expressed being passionately committed to bringing about peace in this world (also the vision of the Modern Mystery School). She had set one of her Tangible, Measurable Results as obtaining clarity about her next step in life. During our ten-month process, she discovered within herself a certainty that she was to go back to school to become a certified midwife. She had been struggling with decisions around where to go next in her life, and there it was, a clear vision of herself as a midwife and the desire to carry that through.

She later told me that she wanted to bring the Baby Blessing, a very powerful energy healing from the lineage of King Salomon to these new humans. Talk about changing the world! (Five of our grandchildren have received this healing and I can tell you firsthand that they are different in all of the right ways!!) This woman now had a purpose, which went well beyond anything she could have imagined. It is certainly birthing of a different kind.

FREEDOM

A young man shared that, during Kabbalah, he was able to quit drinking and abusing drugs, which had become a daily habit. He also left the familiar comfort of his job in a restaurant to pursue and obtain a job in architecture, his field of study in college. This all happened in ten months. Incredible!

Living Kabbalah means responding to the yearnings of our soul and having the energy and tools to follow through on creating the life of our dreams.

AUTHENTICITY

Another exquisite woman gained clarity about her sexual orientation during the course of Kabbalah. She came into the realization that she was, in fact, bisexual and allowed herself to be open to relationships with women as well as men. She came out to the group and was greeted with great love, acceptance and encouragement to follow the path of knowing herself more authentically.

During the first weekend of the next ten-month Kabbalah journey, she introduced her new girlfriend, who was experiencing Kabbalah for the first time and who shared a common hunger for spiritual growth and development. She was living life at a whole new level.

I don't know what her Tangible, Measurable Results were, but I do know that she looked radiantly happy and much freer than she had appeared when we began the journey.

MIRACLES

We saw another example of the magical transformations of Kabbalah in a young man who was looking for fulfillment in his career as an architect and builder. He was unhappy in his present job, in which he was working for someone else. During the ascension process of Universal Kabbalah, he gained clarity that he really would not be able to do what he felt called to do while being employed by someone else.

In those ten months, he put together a plan to work for himself with two partners. The next part is particularly amazing. He had a life dream, well before Kabbalah, of building a design by a world-renowned architect who had, unfortunately, died. Shortly after he joined forces with these other men, they approached him and told him that they had the last plans drafted by the architect he so admired and asked him if he would be interested in a building project utilizing those plans. He was dumbfounded.

Think about this for a moment. By following his soul path through Kabbalah, he not only positioned himself for success, but also had the plans for a structure that was a life-long dream dropped into his lap...from an architect who was dead. How do these things happen! Miraculously!

Crazy right! Crazy Kabbalah, I say.

This is what living Kabbalah looks like for those who embark on the journey and use the tools they are given.

What dream do you have for yourself? What does your soul yearn for? What does your ideal life look like?

What are your Tangible, Measurable Results?

In the next chapter, we will go deeper into what Universal Kabbalah is and how it works so that you can have a deeper understanding of what living Kabbalah is all about.

Tools of Transformation
TANGIBLE, MEASURABLE RESULTS

SETTLE IN

Sit down somewhere that is quiet and where you will not be disturbed.

Sit down with your back well supported, your feet on the floor and your hands in your lap in a receptive position.

Put the tip of your tongue on the roof of your mouth.

BREATHE

Begin by taking a deep breath in through your nose and out through your mouth.

Do this two more times and give yourself permission to relax.

As you continue to breathe and relax, imagine that each breath in contains peace and love.

And now, imagine that each breath out expels all negativity and stress.

Continue this for five to ten minutes.

IMAGINE

Begin to form a picture of your ideal life. Dream BIG.

See this world take shape.

Just breathe and relax for five minutes as the picture comes into focus.

Engage your senses as you develop this picture of your dream.

Then ask yourself the following questions to clarify your picture:

How am I feeling right now?

What are the physical sensations?

What did I hear, taste, smell, sense and feel as I allowed myself to relax and contemplate my ideal life?

WRITE

Describe your ideal life.

Construct three Tangible, Measurable Results that will bring you closer to your dreams.

You may want to utilize the P.M.S. method of writing these TMR's. (Positive, Measurable, Specific)

Write or draw them with intention in this book and on a three by five card and place it somewhere that you will see it every day.

The key to creating your own destiny lies within your heart.

Dig deep and open the door to your Tangible, Measurable Results.

Begin here.

You did it! Come along and I will share with you more manifestations of dreams and goals.

CHAPTER 2

Kabbalah and the Tree of Life

The Tree of Life is growing where the Spirit never dies and the bright light of salvation shines in dark and empty skies.

—BOB DYLAN

In 2007, life took an unexpected turn. One morning at 3:30 a.m., I was awakened by a familiar and loving internal voice. The voice gently invited me for a "visit" downstairs in my family room. Dream-like, I walked downstairs to find the room seemingly unoccupied and yet filled with an unearthly vibrancy and peace. I knew from previous encounters in my childhood that I was in the presence of Jesus. This was the

One who had not only kept me alive during my abuse as a child, but had miraculously healed me of a very serious drug addiction at nineteen.

These incredible encounters happened most mornings for more than six months and then, periodically, over the next few years. During one of these visitations, Jesus said, "Do not be afraid of Kabbalah." This was the first time I ever heard the word Kabbalah. I had forgotten about this message from Jesus until recently when, in order to write this book, I went through the notes I had taken during the time of these visitations.

Words are inadequate to describe the experience of meeting regularly with Jesus, but I can tell you that it was, and is, life-changing. Not only did I question my sanity during this time, but also the safe little world of my "truths" got blown into smithereens. This first visit began a sojourn into the disorienting world of mysticism. Later in the book, I write more about these experiences. I share this here to say that, until thirteen years ago, I had never heard the word Kabbalah.

You may have heard of Kabbalah as a reference to Jewish mysticism or, like me thirteen years ago, have never heard of it. My first exposure to this unusual word was during these visitations. I had no idea what Jesus was talking about. It wasn't until I took a two-day class called Empower Thyself that I was introduced to the concept or even had a frame of reference in which to put it. So, here is a very brief introduction for you to define some terms and give the content of this book a framework.

Kabbalah translates as "to receive" and is a method for navigating life that has been used for thousands of years by the wisest and most successful people on the planet. The Universal Kabbalah is a pure system of inner discovery and practical experience that utilizes all aspects of Kabbalah without being tied to any particular religious affiliation or orthodox dogmas. Carl Jung, Albert Einstein, Nikola Tesla and Leonardo Da Vinci are a few examples of Kabbalists in history.

As stated on the Modern Mystery School website:

> *The Universal Kabbalah is the purest form of esoteric study available in the world today. It is the study of God and the God essence within humans - a noble and essential part of our spiritual inheritance." It is a system of receiving the information embedded in our DNA, often referred to as the Tree of Life. It helps one to understand questions like:*
>
> *Who am I?*
>
> *What am I?*
>
> *Where did I come from?*
>
> *Where am I going?*
>
> *What is my Purpose?*

Here is a list of some of the results of Universal Kabbalah (cited from the Modern Mystery School's publications):

What Kabbalah Will Do for You

1. *Change the way you think from negative thinking to positive thinking.*
2. *Eliminate the subconscious, which constantly bites you in the behind with things from the past.*
3. *Reorganize your mind to eliminate mind clutter. You will accomplish more.*
4. *Re-establish your contact with God and the Hierarchy of Light.*
5. *Awaken your gifts that you have from birth, from God, and your desire to use them.*
6. *Awaken the spiritual aspect of yourself so that you will feel closer to the service to light.*
7. *Set forces in motion that otherwise have been dormant, and these forces will change your life!*

Kabbalah is such a rich and deep path of self-discovery that you could not explore all the treasures that are within you in this lifetime. I have personally experienced all of the results listed above and have witnessed others experiencing them as well. Who doesn't want to be more positive, accomplish more and have a closer connection to our divine self and God? I'll bet you do. I can almost move beyond linear time and space to feel your desire for more as I write this.

THE MODERN MYSTERY SCHOOL

My introduction to Universal Kabbalah came through the Modern Mystery School, which is, well, a mystery to most people. So, I want to tell you a little bit about this ancient school of metaphysics to give you some information.

What is a mystery school? My understanding, after eight years of experiencing and exploring, is that a mystery school is a repository for ancient wisdom teachings, which have been held in sacred trust for all of humanity, to aid in our spiritual progression.

There are seven major ancient mystery schools in the world, and only one is open to the public. That one is the Modern Mystery School, which was opened to the world in 1997 through the amazing dedication and courage of its founder, Baron Gudni Halldor Gudnason von Thoroddsen. This mystery school holds the keys from the lineage of King Salomon and has centers throughout the world. The mission of the Modern Mystery School is simple, yet profound: world peace, or Shamballa, heaven on earth. Isn't that awesome!

UNIVERSAL KABBALAH

One of the paths for spiritual progression that a person can follow in the Modern Mystery School is that of Universal Kabbalah, which I am experiencing for the third time this year. Unlike other Universal Kabbalah classes, this system, put together by the Modern Mystery School, includes an alchemical process of four ascensions during the journey.

This allows us to live the Tree of life, not just learn about it. I experienced visceral shifts in my energy and body. This is deeply satisfying to the soul and allows us to evolve and expand not only during the ten months of the class, but well beyond.

Having been a psychotherapist for twenty-six years, I have not encountered any modality that so completely brings the negative ego to light. Once we know what is there (Know Thyself), we can then choose differently, and not be a slave to our subconscious. As I said earlier, Kabbalah does more for personal growth than ten years of intense therapy. I am living proof of that.

Imagine becoming aware of a process that is lying quietly, but dynamically, within every fiber of our being and contains within it a map for a path to peace. Kabbalah is that map and it is available to all of humanity.

For some great information on this, watch the video by Eric Thompson on my website, https://empoweredliving.academy. He is one of my teachers and an international instructor for the Modern Mystery School.

THE TREE OF LIFE

The Tree of Life is the roadmap for Kabbalah, and it is used in various mystical traditions. In his book, *The Complete Guide to the Kabbalah,* Will Parfitt writes, "At the heart of Western Mystery Tradition, the Kabbalah is a way of personal development and self-realization based on a map of consciousness called the Tree of Life. The Tree of Life can be used to express self-realization through a vision of love and harmony."

The Hermetic Tree consists of ten spheres containing different archetypes and correspondences and twenty-two lines connecting the spheres. The circles, also referred to as sephiroth, are arranged into three columns or pillars.

While the sephiroth are represented as circles, the lines represent paths. The sephiroth represent different aspects of existence, God, and the human psyche. The lines represent the relationship between these concepts. The spheres have many correspondences such as the different names of God, archangels, angels, celestial bodies, vices and virtues/values and so much more.

THE TREE OF LIFE

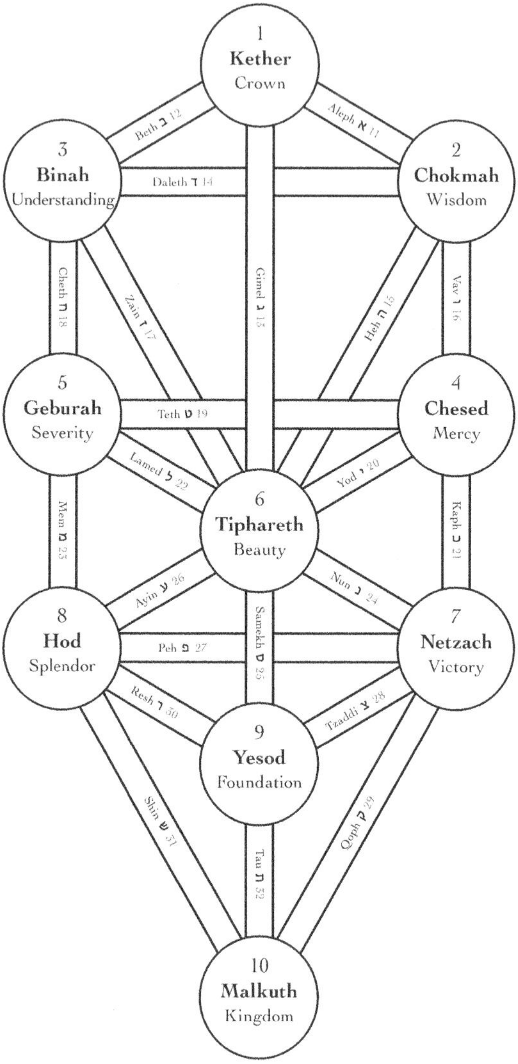

THE TREE OF LIFE WITHIN THE HUMAN BODY

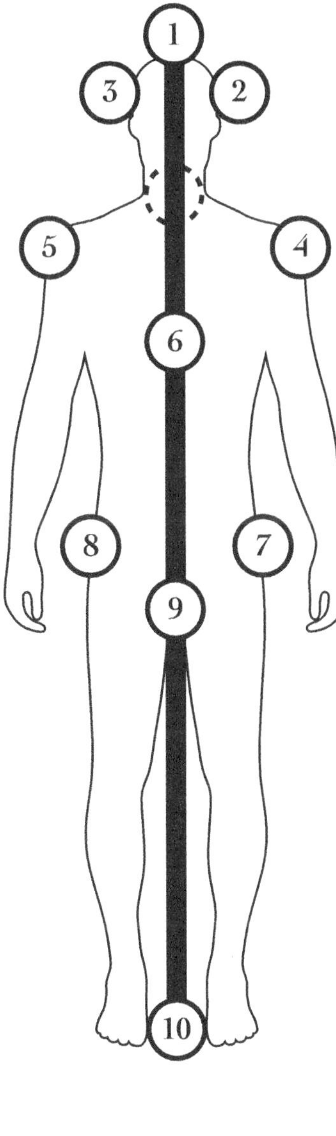

TREE OF LIFE DIAGRAMS

One way we use this Tree of Life is to weave the energies of the left and right pillars while centering ourselves on the middle pillar. The tools provided through the Modern Mystery School tradition help us to navigate this journey.

Essentially, the Tree of Life is a way of identifying particular energetic structures that are found in all of creation, from the microcosm of our cells to the macrocosm of the universe. And it is filled with mysteries waiting to be uncovered. Imagine it as something that is imprinted in our bodies that orients us to our divine destination. It is the Universe's proof to us that the Creator is always working for our greater good and the good of humanity.

Now that you are more familiar with the process of Kabbalah, as well as with the Tree of Life (the map that guides us through the Kabbalah experience), we will explore, in the next chapter, more of what the experience of living Kabbalah is like.

Tools of Transformation
THE TREE OF LIFE

SETTLE IN

Sit down somewhere that is quiet and where you will not be disturbed.

Sit down with your back well supported, your feet on the floor and your hands in your lap in a receptive position.

Put the tip of your tongue on the roof of your mouth behind your front teeth.

BREATHE

Begin by taking a deep breath in through your nose and out through your mouth.

Do this two more times and give yourself permission to relax.

Follow your breath for the next ten minutes.

IMAGINE

As you continue to breathe and relax, take the images of the Tree of Life into your mind's eye.

Contemplate these images for five minutes.

See what comes up for you.

You may begin to feel the power of this structure and its influence in your life. Ask yourself these questions:

How am I feeling right now?

What did I hear, taste, smell, sense and feel as I allowed myself to contemplate these images?

WRITE

Use the space in this book, or use your own notebook, to journal answers to these questions.

Let yourself write until there is nothing more to write.

If you cannot think of anything to write, then begin by drawing the Tree of Life. Draw it ten times. How did that feel?

The key to the Tree of Life lies within.

Let it blossom by beginning here.

Awesome! Your Awakening to the Tree has begun.

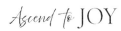

CHAPTER 3

Kabbalah as a Powerful Journey

If you are always trying to be normal,
you will never know how amazing you can be.

—MAYA ANGELOU

The room was buzzing with excitement as people from all over the world settled down to begin class. To the right of me was a physician from South Africa, to the left, an accomplished Canadian martial artist. In the back was a young mother from Ireland with babe in arms as well as a former Navy Seal. This eclectic and talented group of over 100 people had gathered to learn from one of the greatest teachers of Universal Kabbalah in the world.

Front and center was Founder Gudni Gudnason, our teacher and one of the most accomplished and gifted men I have ever met. Flanking him were two amazing women, Dr. Theresa Bullard, a physicist from California, and Verla Wade, a very successful corporate trainer and businesswoman from Seattle.

What was I, a grandmother from Michigan, doing among this incredible group of people? Three short years before, I didn't even know Kabbalah existed.

My Guide from the Modern Mystery School, Barbara Segura, had invited me to take Universal Kabbalah in Toronto, Ontario in Canada, which was about a four-hour drive from our home in Royal Oak, Michigan. I had been through some pretty significant shifts in the previous six months, including a Life Activation and an empowering weekend ending in an initiation into something called the Brotherhood and Sisterhood of Light in the lineage of King Salomon. Pretty unusual for a Catholic school girl in her sixtieth year of life, to say the least.

At the start of this class experience, we were invited to set goals in terms of Tangible, Measurable Results, which we would work toward accomplishing during the ten months of the class. I remember the dream board I created in general terms, but not the specifics. What I do remember very clearly is the life-changing shift I experienced during the course of the class, and how this shift would see me through some potentially life-shattering events.

LIFE WAS GOOD

Part of the Universal Kabbalah experience, as designed and presented by the Modern Mystery School, involves an alchemical process, from my understanding, that allows the participant opportunities to shed old patterns of behavior and thought patterns. This clears the way for new attitudes and thoughts that bring about a more authentic understanding and expression of the self.

At this point in my life, I had worked really hard at becoming the best version of myself through years of education, work with various twelve-step recovery programs, psychotherapy, spiritual work and developing healthy habits. My efforts had produced a sober and drug-free life after years of addiction to alcohol and drugs, as well as recovery from two eating disorders. My body was the healthiest it had been in years. Life was brighter and I had maintained a one-hundred-fifteen-pound weight loss for almost twenty years. My work was fulfilling, and I was doing what I loved as a psychotherapist in private practice. Life was good!!

DRAMA AND EMOTIONS

And I knew it could be better. You may be at this point in your life as well. That nagging feeling that there is more - more peace, more joy, more love to be lived. Which leads me to sharing with you the transformation that happened to me during the second ascension (the alchemical portion of the class).

To give you a framework for this experience, let me say that, with all the decades of work I had done on myself, I was still not living life with a balance between my logical self and my emotional self. I weighed in heavily on the emotional side with logic taking a definite second. My husband of over forty years could attest to that, for sure. This emotionality and the drama it produced had caused a great deal of discomfort for me and the people around me. Having been diagnosed with Post- Traumatic Stress Disorder (PTSD) as a result of my childhood abuse, I had been living with my reptilian, or survival, brain in charge for too much of the time.

I made it my mission to collect a personal toolbox of awesome and useful tools with which to navigate life in a more balanced way. I did this, deliberately, consciously and with much effort, much, much effort. And I was successful in maintaining a modicum of sanity during most of life's challenges, by and large. The cost is that I lived life with periods of exhaustion and anxiety from the effort.

Does this sound at all familiar? Are there areas of your life that you work so hard at that you become exhausted? Are there periods of time in your life when anxiety and depression are unwelcome guests? I certainly had them. Let me describe for you the moment that all changed.

LIFE TRANSFORMED

To describe the ascension process with words is difficult for me as it was a truly metaphysical experience. I can tell you this, though. It changed me forever.

As I reflect on it, the best way to describe it was that I experienced a visceral, energetic shift. We were in the midst of an ascension exercise facilitated by Founder Gudni, and I felt, and almost heard a *clunk,* in my energy field, somewhat like when the last piece to a mechanical puzzle falls into place and the gears start to whirl. In my mind's eye, I found myself on the middle pillar in the sephira of Tiphareth, and guess who was there? Jesus was there with me. I began internally processing the experience and wondered what it meant. The next couple of months revealed to me (and those around me) that my emotional and logical selves had synced up somehow and were now working together in balance rather than fighting for control.

Since that experience almost six years ago, a balance between my mind and emotions has stayed with me. I recently asked someone who knows me well to describe her experience of me in the last six years, and she said, "You are loving, peaceful and joyful." Yay, Kabbalah! Yay, Tree of Life!! My goal of responding to life's challenges rather than reacting has become almost effortless.

LIVING PROOF

How do I know that? Well, there were two events that tested this balance in ways that I hope you never have to experience. The first was finding out that our eight-year-old grandson, Michael, was diagnosed with a very rare form of leukemia, and the second was the quick and tragic death of one of my dearest friends, also a Michael. These events happened within months of each other and during the time I was taking Universal Kabbalah.

With the discovery of our grandson's illness and all during his five-and-a-half-month hospitalization, I was able to be the grandma he needed me to be, and I wanted to be, without the drama, sleeplessness or hysteria I might have experienced in the past. This was also true during our friend Mike's short, but arduous battle with pancreatic cancer and subsequent death.

Being able to be so present with so much less effort was amazing and somewhat disconcerting to me. I actually checked in with my husband and my friend, Barbara, both of whom have been therapists themselves, to see if I was somehow dissociating or numbing myself to these experiences. They assured me that I was not. They could verify that the shift I had experienced was a healthier version of myself. And this shift has lasted right up to today, five years later.

This is the new me. The Universal Kabbalah experience had achieved more for me in minutes than I had been able to achieve with many years of pretty intensive therapy. Crazy, right? No, crazy Kabbalah!

WHAT IN YOURSELF OR YOUR LIFE WOULD YOU LIKE TO CHANGE?

Do you want a clearer idea of your purpose in life?

Do you want employment that is more in alignment with your purpose?

Do you want a loving relationship with a partner or improvements in the relationships you have in your family, friendships or work?

Do you desire better health?

Are you looking for a resolution to a particular problem?

Let's take some time to really meditate on these questions and see what comes to the surface.

Tools of Transformation
EMBRACING AND RELEASING

SETTLE IN

Sit down somewhere that is quiet and where you will not be disturbed.

Sit down with your back well supported, your feet on the floor and your hands in your lap in a receptive position.

Put the tip of your tongue on the roof of your mouth behind your front teeth.

BREATHE

Begin by taking a deep breath in through your nose and out through your mouth.

Do this two more times and give yourself permission to relax.

Continue this method for another ten minutes.

IMAGINE

As you continue to breathe and relax, imagine that each breath in contains peace and love.

And now imagine that each breath out expels all negativity and stress.

Continue breathing in this way, taking the life force energy of your breath deep into your belly, and completely expelling all negativity.

How would I like to change my way of being in the world?

Imagine yourself in the way that you would ideally show up in life. Really imagine it.

Imagine all aspects of your life physically, emotionally, mentally, socially and spiritually.

See yourself in your highest way of being, and then imagine what that would look like.

Close your eyes. Breathe. Continue to relax.

WRITE

Write down three things that you would like to change in yourself.

Use the space in this book, or use your own notebook, to journal the following:

How am I feeling right now?

What are the physical sensations?

What did I hear, taste, smell, sense and feel as I allowed myself to relax?

What does my desired self look like? Feel Like?

Write your answers down or draw a picture in the space provided on the next 2 pages.

The key to who you really are is here.

Take the next step and begin to bring into focus who that is, beginning now.

Well done. Creating a picture of yourself and your ideal life is the first step to manifesting the life of your dreams.

CHAPTER 4

Asking Ourselves the Right Questions

It is not that we don't know the right answers,
it is that we don't ask the right questions.

—TONY ROBBINS

Do you ever question yourself? Have you ever thought about questioning those questions? One of the tools we learn to use in Universal Kabbalah is asking ourselves the right questions. You see, the journey that is illuminated during Kabbalah is a journey of the soul. Because the soul is the interface between the spirit and the body, there are definite physical results alongside the spiritual results. And the process involves the deeper questions of life, which are worth mentioning again.

They are:
Who am I?
What am I?
Where did I come from?
Where am I going?
What is my purpose?

It is in seeking the answers to these questions that we see the movement of the Holy Spirit (Higher Self) rearranging our lives according to the goals of the soul. Pretty cool, eh?

It also helps us to determine if what we think we want is what we really need. Asking the right questions will lead us to uncover the deeper answers. This is a path that is deeply satisfying to the soul.

Universal Kabbalah's final weekend includes each participant sharing some of their Tangible, Measurable Results through various creative expressions, whether that be through writing, art, music, a slide presentation or any other form of creativity. Let's look at some of the Tangible, Measurable Results that came from asking the right questions by members of my second Kabbalah group. Ready for a fun ride?

WHO AM I?

Let's start with a young woman who asked herself the question: *Who am I?* In the beginning of the ten-month journey, she reported being a very insecure, people pleasing person who was ruled by family and friends.

As she progressed into each section of our study, or aspect of herself in this case, I watched as her relationships melted away or, in some circumstances, blew up. She was stripping away the codependent parts of her life, sometimes painfully and with great trepidation.

Alongside this grew a self-confidence and awareness of who she was as a divine being. Imagine our surprise as she presented to the group her final project - a motorcycle helmet! She had bought a Harley and was riding it with flair! Her beautifully decorated helmet was the symbol of the fearlessness and adventure that had been missing from her life. She had been riddled with fears for most of her life by her report. She not only faced her fear, but persevered through the rejection of friends and family and stepped into her power. She came to realize that living Kabbalah, for her, meant big changes and the Kabbalah experience gave her the ability to make those changes.

WHAT AM I?

The second powerful question we ask in Kabbalah is: *What am I?* We saw the power of this question in the life of a beautifully, emerging artist and author who discovered what she was during the Kabbalah journey. This woman had such a heart of service and created elegant altars while transforming rooms in hotels and retreat centers into sacred spaces of beauty for all of us.

Her creativity also produced the Tangible, Measurable Result of creating a children's book that introduces metaphysical principles in a delightful and engaging way. Upon completion, I hope to see a copy in every school. Her illustrations are alive and expressive, just like her.

To find what she truly is, she went through a purifying process of leaving her job and getting another. She added to her identity as an accomplished professional, a more authentic piece of herself as author and illustrator and creator of sacred space. Such is the process of Kabbalah: eliminating that which does not serve us any longer and activating those parts of us that will lead us to God, that will lead us to ourselves.

Now, she is pursuing the path of becoming a Guide within the Modern Mystery School and helping others in their spiritual progression. And that is what living Kabbalah is all about - our spiritual progression. Now when she asks herself, *What am I?*, these have become her answers: I am a Guide, a teacher, a healer, an author and an illustrator. This is the direct result of asking the right questions and the soul responding through Kabbalah.

Another young woman stood up at the end of our journey and said that for the first time in her life she had been described as "happy, joyous and upbeat" and that she realized it was true. She had walked into Kabbalah looking very depressed and angry. *What am I?* In her words she said, "Ten years ago, I would have been described as a mean, unhappy bitch. You have helped me to see the real me." As a psychotherapist for twenty-six years who has worked with thousands of people, I can tell you that changing someone's image of themselves is a long, arduous process. Imagine, all this in ten months. Magic or miracle?

What would you like to change in your life? What if that change could happen in less than a year?

WHAT IS MY PURPOSE?

Another dynamic woman, with a never-ending effervescence, brought forth a Tangible, Measurable Result as we were sitting at the dinner table during our final weekend. She had been asking herself, *What is my purpose in life?* After I presented excerpts from my book during class, Heather came over to the table and offered to be my editor. She was so excited because something that had been germinating in her had smacked her in her beautiful face at that moment. "I am supposed to edit books and find, or create, a publishing company that publishes books on spirituality and metaphysics." And that is exactly what she is doing!

Directly after the final session of this Kabbalah class, she met a friend of a friend who (you guessed it) owns a publishing company whose mission is to publish books that raise the vibration of the planet. She now works for O'Leary Publishing and is my editor... and friend... and sister. (How fortunate am I?)

In fact, I just got a text from her yesterday checking in on my writing, which ironically enough had come to a halt.

I told her as much, and this was the text that she sent back to me:

> *Sometimes these breaks are the bamboo plant growing roots. It is needed for the creative process. All in divine timing!*

She was reminding me of something we had learned from Eric, our Kabbalah teacher. He had told us the story of the Chinese bamboo plant, which takes five years of incubation to grow roots before finally breaking through the earth. Imagine, for five years, there is no outward sign of growth! And then, the bamboo plant grows up to sixty feet or more in only five weeks. But it can only do this because it has grown a very solid root system or foundation.

This reminder, and words of encouragement, from my editor helped me move my thinking from being "stuck" to incubation, and that was just what I needed. Because of this, I was once again inspired to write. So, here I am on the train to Toronto, at 5:30 in the morning, writing once again. Believe me, there is nothing like having an editor who is also living Kabbalah.

I understand, now, that our Kabbalah instructor's purpose in asking us to create Tangible, Measurable Results was to help us see the movement of Spirit in our lives. As we align our will with the Will of God, we are intentional and approach life with an open mind and a full heart. The adage, "seeing is believing," definitely works here as we watched these important changes happen over and over again in one another.

Some of the TMRs were shared through PowerPoint and slide presentations. I watched as one woman showed us the evolving process of creating an organic, locally sourced restaurant that she charmingly decorated to create an ambience of peace and tranquility. And this she did on the tails of a debilitating illness. I felt tears come to my eyes at the slides of her restaurant's opening and all the joy that was exhibited. What is her purpose in life? I would say to create goodness and beauty in the world.

WHERE AM I GOING?

Another pictorial presentation took us down the road of a man who magically moved into his first home. He is a professional actor who up to this point had not put down roots. Ganesha was a very meaningful spiritual figure to him, and when he stepped into this house for the first time, a waist high statue of Ganesha stood at the front door. Sign after sign presented themselves and he knew without a doubt that this was home. The message was clear. *Where am I going?* I'm going home, both on the physical and the metaphysical plains.

More importantly, in this case, I witnessed the opening of this man coming home to himself as he revealed his heart. He discarded the mask of guardedness and began engaging people from a more authentic place, warm and loving. How beautiful!! He was living Kabbalah in ways that led him to this divine expression of himself. I recently spoke with him and was, again, struck by the depth of his presence and the beauty of his soul.

A final PowerPoint presentation showed the opening of a powerful woman's healing center, which had been many years in the making. She also stepped into her destiny by apprenticing with Founder Gudni, thus fulfilling the dream of her life.

These are a sample of the Tangible, Measurable Results of Kabbalah, of what happens when we ask ourselves the right questions and what it means to *live* Kabbalah.

AWAKENING TO AUTHENTICITY

In asking the right questions, we become aware of the different levels of creation in life. I was acutely aware of the many levels that were being manifested in this group for the good of the whole. In addition to the personal manifestation of Tangible, Measurable Results, there were the intangible, magical and mystical results within the community of this Kabbalah group.

For me, the greatest result of this journey through Kabbalah was the co-creation of a community built on love and acceptance. "And the greatest of these is *love*" (1 Corinthians 13:13). We manifested this through vulnerability and lowering our masks, and it was forged out of faith in the Tree of Life that God created within us and in each other. Imagine the microcosm of this process developing into the macrocosm of all of society.

Can you feel it? Ordinary people from all walks of life with an extraordinary connection through the Tree of Life, which awakens who they truly are. Imagine a world in which each person uncovers his or her real, authentic self, sees and affirms the divinity in everyone and honors our connectedness. Imagine if what we saw in ourselves and others fed a fountain of love that never dried up. You got it. World peace. Enough for everyone. No fears, no worries, no anger. No doubt that we are all in this together. No judgments but, instead, an appreciation of all expressions of goodness and beauty.

Please, do not think this was an adventure of daisies and unicorns farting rainbows. Sometimes, the answers to these awesome questions are painful and stretch our capacity for change to the max. We become afraid of the unknown and of pruning the Tree within us. But this pruning is needed so that we will produce good fruit. As one in our group described this journey, it is like a massive rollercoaster ride that climbs with the sound of grinding gears and reaches the peak, at which time you think, "Let me get off!" only to go plummeting to the earth. Disembarking, you let out an exultant cry and scurry to the end of the line to get back on because you had so much fun!

Welcome to Universal Kabbalah Park, the adventure of a lifetime! And guess what? This is my third time on this ride, and I look forward to the next one. Will you be on it with me? Whether you want to birth your own dreams or fly on the adventure of a lifetime, Kabbalah has the keys. You don't have to believe what I believe, but, if you want what I want, which is to know myself authentically and to have world peace, then pick up the map and climb the Tree. I'll be right alongside you.

Begin by asking the right questions.

Tools of Transformation
ASKING THE RIGHT QUESTIONS

SETTLE IN

Sit down somewhere that is quiet and where you will not be disturbed.

Sit down with your back well supported, your feet on the floor and your hands in your lap in a receptive position.

Put the tip of your tongue on the roof of your mouth behind your front teeth.

BREATHE

Begin taking a deep breath in through your nose and out through your mouth.

Do this two more times and give yourself permission to relax.

Continue this breathing as you answer the five following questions, taking your time for each one.

IMAGINE

Try not to filter what comes to you.

Take three breaths, relax and then say the question out loud.

Who am I?

Drop into your heart as you answer.

What am I?

Let your soul answer the question.

Where did I come from?

Where am I going?

What is my purpose?

Open your senses, both physically and psychically.

WRITE

Write about or draw your experience of asking yourself these questions.

Anchor in the experience with your journaling.

What did you discover?

The most important journey one can make is to Know Thyself.

I challenge you to begin now. I would love to hear what you find.

Write your answers down or draw a picture in the space provided on the next 2 pages.

The key to life is asking the right questions.

To Know Thyself begin here.

Try doing this exercise for thirty days and see what shifts inside of you and in your life.

CHAPTER 5

Rewriting Our Past: Debugging the Divine Program

The first draft of anything is shit.

—ERNEST HEMINGWAY

Working with computers can be so frustrating sometimes. We use specific programs to get certain results. When there is a bug in the program, it not only doesn't produce what we are looking for, but also can disrupt and corrupt other aspects of our work. Life is like that sometimes. We are living our daily lives and run into reactions in ourselves that sabotage what we are trying to accomplish.

Debugging is the step-by-step process of finding errors in a program so that we can remove the bugs. This allows the program to function in the way it was designed. What if there was an effective and efficient way to change our programming? To change our reactions into responses and eliminate unnecessary drama from our lives?

Kabbalah is the *divine* debugger. My journey through Kabbalah shifted my perception of my childhood experiences and allowed me to see myself, and my personal history, from a more loving, compassionate perspective. This *debugging* has changed everything. The shift has cleared the way for more self-love and love for my parents.

I recently discovered my mother's journals relaying events from when I was a child. Reading my mother's experiences drastically changed my perception of my childhood and thus, my perception of myself.

PERSPECTIVE

Our perception is our reality at that moment. You have probably seen the black and white picture used by psychologists where you can see either a face of an old woman, or the image of a young woman. How does that happen? Well, what we see depends upon where we focus. What if you could radically change your focus? Kabbalah has a way of doing this for us.

CHAPTER 5

WHAT DO YOU SEE?

You are a divine being and the author of your own life, not only today, but in the past and the future. Everything that has happened in your life has contributed to who you are and has meaning and purpose. Join me in the journey of changing my perspective of the past to make way for a more peaceful present and joyful future.

Kabbalah was the vehicle for that transformation by debugging my inner program.

From the ages of four-and-a-half to eight, I was sexually abused and physically tortured by a teenager who lived behind us. I have done a tremendous amount of healing work to address the pain remaining in my psyche from these traumatic years. And yet, I still held a very deep wound from the fact that my parents did not notice the torment I was in during that formative time. After all, they were fairly intelligent people, and I was their oldest child. Why didn't they help me? As a result of this, I felt unloved at a very deep level. That programming followed me into many areas of my life.

As a psychotherapist for twenty-six years, I know it is vitally important that children are seen and heard and kept safe as a foundation for trust and a healthy self-image. Both of these foundational concepts have been a challenge for me for most of my life. Due to my work in Kabbalah, this wounded part of my inner child feels safer and healthier than ever before.

REWRITING CHILDHOOD

This amazing shift for my inner child happened during my last ascension when I found something my mother had written, which gave me a different perspective of this life narrative. Because of this, my belief that my parents didn't love me was transformed, and I was able to rewrite the story of my childhood.

The afternoon I wrote this, I decided to take a break from my writing. I wandered downstairs and found myself in the storage room. I mildly wondered what had drawn me to this room at this time. I was feeling strangely led to go through some old papers, purging and cleaning an old file cabinet - a wonderful metaphor for the process I was experiencing in Kabbalah. All of this occurred while I was in a relaxed state of mind.

Inside the file cabinet, I found notes that my parents wrote in 1980 during a marriage retreat. I truly have no memory of having received these notebooks, and I was surprised to read the following passage written by my mother:

> *One of the most difficult years of my life was 1956 - I was 27 years old. I had an uncomfortable pregnancy and when I was 6 ¾ months pregnant, I started hemorrhaging and went into labor at the same time. I gave birth to twin boys who died shortly after. I felt so betrayed. This sort of thing happened to others. Not me. I was healthy and had good pregnancies. I had lost much blood, had a transfusion and was sent home in 5 days. Depression – I asked God over and over, Why? I sat and rocked my 9-month-old baby Angel [my sister Diane] and cried and cried. Shortly after, Jim's 16-year-old cousin, not married, gave birth to twin boys also, the same weight as mine (3 1/2 and 4 pounds) and they lived. I was anxious and bitter. We wanted another baby right away, so I was pregnant in April but miscarried in August - more tears and depression. Jim was comforting but I did not think I could have another baby. I got pregnant in October, spent an anxious and careful 9 months and gave birth to a healthy baby boy.*

My mother went on to have six more children after that!

I was rocked to my core. Here was my very young mother, severely depressed and spending hours and hours rocking my sister to find some sort of consolation. My heart went out to her.

I then remembered my father. Throughout the years, people asked him how he could be so positive. He explained that when he found out that my mother was having twins and that he would have five children under the age of five, he panicked. He explained that he went to God and said, "How am I going to support this family? How could you do this to me?"

When the twins died, he said he felt tremendous remorse and promised God that he would be grateful not only for his children, but also for all the things that life brought his way. And, by and large, he was!

During the time of the twins' deaths, however, he was almost paralyzed and could only manage to get to work and back, according to a story he told me later. I remember the pain in his face and the frozen tears in his eyes when he recounted this story to me. He resolved to work as many hours as he could to support his family. I only knew that he was never home.

These insights into my parents brought tremendous healing and comfort to me. This was not about whether I was lovable or not. This was about their own pain and suffering.

As a mother myself, I had wondered how they could miss my sudden fearfulness and withdrawal much less the multitude of bruises and cuts on my little body. Now I had the clear and indisputable proof that they couldn't see what was happening to me because they were entrenched in their own sorrows and tragedies. They were so young and had so many responsibilities. My family had been very child-centered in so many ways that, up to this moment, their blindness made no sense to me. Now I understood.

I immediately felt release and freedom from my resentment, confusion and self-image of someone completely unlovable by her parents. The bug in my personal lovability program disappeared, and I was restored to the Divine Program. I am completely loved.

So, there I was, at the edge of the abyss, feeling an incredible compassion and forgiveness in a whole new way for my parents. I redefined the story of my childhood from *I was a child who was so unimportant to her parents that they ignored her in a time of great harm to I was a loved and treasured child.*

In addition to this amazing transformation, that same day, I opened an email for a daily devotional, and this is what it said:

> *I am opening a new chapter in your life. The last chapter is over and done, and the conclusions are no longer relevant. Position yourself to step into what I have prepared for you. Step into the newness of life in the Spirit. Rise above your history and be done with regrets and condemnation, says the Lord.*
>
> —*Marsha Burns, Faith Tabernacle of Kremmling*

Synchronicity? Perhaps. When I was a high school religion teacher in the late 1970's, I had a bulletin board that said, "Coincidences are miracles in which God wishes to remain anonymous."

The Divine Program which is embedded in my DNA - Divine Nature Always - is my truth, and Kabbalah has the ability to debug programs that don't serve that purpose.

DEBUGGING OUR PROGRAMS

What in your own personal history affects your thoughts, feelings and decisions today? It may have been a trauma, but it could also have been a decision you made as a result of something someone said or that you saw. That decision may have made its way into a core belief and is lying in the unconscious, acting as an engineer and constructing your life without your conscious consent.

A way to identify these bugs is to use the acronym ANT. This stands for Automatic Negative Thoughts. They are one of the results of faulty programming. They will keep you viewing life from the worm's eye view, keeping your face in the mud. What if you could see things from a completely different point of view? The eagle's eye view.

The following exercise will help you to begin to debug your programming and start to rid yourself of the ANTs. It is important to really relax before beginning and ask your Higher Self, or the God of your understanding, for help in bringing the bugs in your subconscious to the surface. Ask for help to identify those parts of your program that are not Divine. The following exercise will help you identify when your negative programming is in overdrive. Be very creative with this and have fun.

Tools of Transformation
DEBUGGING

SETTLE IN

Sit down somewhere that is quiet and where you will not be disturbed.

Sit down with your back well supported, your feet on the floor and your hands in your lap in a receptive position.

Put the tip of your tongue on the roof of your mouth behind your front teeth.

BREATHE

Begin by taking a deep breath in through your nose and out through your mouth.

Do this two more times and give yourself permission to relax.

As you continue to breathe and relax, imagine that each breath in contains peace and love.

And now imagine that each breath out expels all negativity and stress.

Continue breathing in this way, taking the life force energy of your breath deep into your belly and completely expelling all negativity.

IMAGINE

While relaxed, ask the question: What does it sound like when I am talking to myself?

What critical or negative things do I say to myself? These are very likely the bugs.

Imagine these negative thoughts as ANTs (Automatic Negative Thoughts).

Now, with the next breath, imagine your own personal imaginary anteater. Is it male or female? What color is it? Name it. Next, see your ANTs being devoured by your inner anteater.

Use this whenever the negative thoughts appear and see what happens.

WRITE

Take a few moments to write about your experience.

Draw your anteater if that helps. You can use this exercise as a mini meditation each day or as you notice the bugs in your program for Divine Nature Always being corrupted.

Write your answers down or draw a picture in the space provided on the next 2 pages.

The key to rewriting your past is in changing your perspective.

Start to identify the ANTs that are in your way.
Begin now.

Divinely done!! Now let's peek into the possibilities of who you really are.

CHAPTER 6

Transforming Self-Image

You yourself, as much as anybody in the entire universe, deserve your love and affection.

—BUDDHA

Years ago, an ethereal young man stepped into my office. He was tall and slender, with striking blue eyes and a mane of blonde streaked hair. He was slumped over with eyes either downcast or darting all around. He sat silently for a few minutes and then mumbled something under his breath. I told him I couldn't hear him, and he blurted out, "I hate myself." He was all of fifteen years old. He had asked his parents to bring him in because he was having thoughts of harming himself.

Underlying many of the problems that brought people into my office as a psychotherapist was a distorted, inaccurate and negative self-image. Fear, guilt and shame were the toxic threads of their personal tapestry and the unravelling of daily life.

When you tune into the channel of your own self-talk, are you more apt to hear the mind chatter of negativity or the sweet sounds of self-love? Ask yourself the question: Is this how I would speak to those whom I love? What about your self-image? Can you look in the mirror and say, "I love you," without discomfort or looking away? Let's take some time to see how you can transform your thoughts and image of yourself from where you are today to self-love so that you will discover the divine being that you are.

In Kabbalah, as you uncover some deeply embedded negative beliefs you may be holding about yourself, you will find a powerful release when you let them go. The process will continue as you, then, allow space for another layer to rise to the surface. This process is an ongoing journey of self-awareness and a dismembering of the programming that is not serving your Divine higher purpose.

NEGATIVE SELF-IMAGE

For many years of my adult life, there were mornings when I looked in the mirror and believed that I was fat, dumb and ugly. Getting dressed, I would look in the mirror and see my body and feel uncomfortable in my clothing. My thinking was cloudy and unclear, and I focused on the parts of me that I did not like. Sounds pretty harsh, doesn't it?

I believed I was fat way before I really was obese. I had lots of proof. Decades before, I overheard my mother talking to some of my female relatives saying, "Chrissy has such a pretty face but…" as her voice trailed off and her face looked sad. This moment repeated often.

In the fifth grade, I loomed over most of my classmates, both girls and boys. At five feet, seven inches tall, weighing 150 lbs. and wearing a size 36C bra, I felt betrayed by my body as I drew unwanted attention. I was an eleven-year-old child in a woman's body, and, to add insult to injury, I began my period before my eleventh birthday.

The supermodel of the day when I was in high school went by the name Twiggy. Looking back, I feel great compassion for someone who probably had an eating disorder, but, at the time, I envied her boyish figure, gaunt face and lack of hips or breasts. I was a girl with lots of curves and the sturdy and substantial thighs of my heritage as a German farmer's daughter. No Twiggy by any stretch of the imagination.

Also, as a result of my sexual abuse history, I was loath to attract any male attention that was sexual in nature. The paradox was that I often dressed provocatively, although I am rethinking that perception even as I write. I mean, how provocative can you be in a Catholic school uniform under the scrutiny of the nuns!

The script that frequently played in my mind, that I was not smart, came from many sources. Memorizing anything was incredibly difficult although I could recount personal conversations from years before word for word. Knowing what I know now about childhood trauma and the development of the brain, it makes sense that my memory, both long-term and short, was sketchy and undependable.

My decision-making and spatial abilities were compromised which were markers of the struggle my brain had in developing fully. It was also difficult for me to keep myself in the present moment as I often got lost in the past. Yes, most people have problems staying in the moment, but this was a form of dissociation that was not normal.

I also remember my father trying to help me with my math homework and finally ending the session in frustration saying, "If only you were more logical!" This happened with regularity.

That explains my fat and dumb programming, but how about feeling ugly?

Although my husband once described me as the all-American girl next door when he first met me, I saw myself as inadequate and lacking in the looks department. One of the boys in my childhood neighborhood group gave me the nickname, "Two-Ton Tessy." And it stuck.

The popular conception of beauty in my day was to be very thin. I had curves. I was constantly comparing myself to other girls, and I didn't like the girl I saw in the mirror. My internal mantra was, *Not good enough.*

I continued to grow spiritually throughout adulthood, and I knew, in my heart of hearts, that my perception of myself was inaccurate and harmful. Even before discovering Kabbalah, one of my daily prayers was, "Dear God, please help me to see myself through Your eyes." My heart saw beauty everywhere except in the mirror.

I could not see the "Beauty of the Divine Expression," another truth about self from Kabbalah, that was within me.

THE WOMAN IN THE CORNER

This began to change when I started meditating at nineteen, shortly after a miraculous reprieve from a drug addiction, which was one of the ways I dealt with my abuse history and resulting low self-esteem. Meditation became a practice that brought me a modicum of peace and, I am certain, a way for my brain and nervous system to heal. In fact, I am sure that this daily practice saved me from a lot of suffering. It empowered me to harness my mind and my negative ego and install a "pause-button" when life seemed out of control.

Many years ago, I put a special chair for meditation in my office, which was a safe haven for me. This spot is still my favorite place to meditate. At the time of this event, I was at a stage in my prayer and meditation practice in which I spent time in za-zen (sitting meditation) and time in intercessory prayer (praying on another's behalf). I would sit quietly, and, after a time, I would have a distinct impression of someone for whom I needed to pray.

One morning, I entered into my meditation and had the experience of being able to envision someone standing just inside the door of my "womb room," which is what I called my office and meditation room at the time. She was tall, slender and very powerful looking. She radiated the energy of love and was quite beautiful. She emitted a sense of wisdom, and I was drawn to her. I did not recognize her, although there was a vague familiarity about her.

I suspected that this woman was the one I was to pray for and wondered who she was. I wondered if she was a political figure or someone who needed prayer support in making a big decision.

I went to my "inner beach," a place in my mind where I sit with Jesus and listen, and asked who she was. During this practice, I generally just sat on the sand next to Him, my shoulder touching His as we looked out over the water. He turned to me with what I would describe as a mischievous grin, and I realized, in a flash, that she was me as He saw me!

Now, mind you, the woman that was me, sitting in the chair at that time, some thirty years ago, weighed 250 lbs. and was convinced that she was not only fat, but also dumb and ugly as well. Although I could not fully embrace this revelation at the time, it gave me a different perspective, a possibility that did not exist for me before. It became a beacon to follow for the next thirty years. I had a window into the "Beauty of the Divine Expression" that was me!

That light led me through surgery, a complete diet and lifestyle change and the vision of who I was in God's eyes. Slowly but surely, I shed over one hundred pounds and became strong, balanced and flexible. If only the old thought patterns had kept up with the physical changes. And that is where Kabbalah stepped in.

Me in my larger rental vehicle.

"Queen" size me dancing with my loving husband.

My new vehicle - I chose the sports car version.

A SELF-IMAGE OF DIVINITY & BEAUTY

Today at sixty-eight years old, at five feet, seven inches and one hundred and thirty-five pounds, I am colorful, bright-eyed and energetically youthful. I know my purpose in life is to bring about world peace in whatever way I can, and that gives me direction and confidence, which others find attractive.

My job description as a Guide in the Modern Mystery School is "to love everyone all of the time." That gives me my North Star. And, as I orient myself toward my purpose and embrace my innate divinity, my body and mind follow suit. I am free from the constant anxiety I once had, and my creative intelligence is working once again. When I look in the mirror now, I clearly see the light in my eyes and smile and know it is radiating from God within me.

TRANSFORMING SELF-IMAGE

More recently, there were three distinct steps that dramatically helped with my negative self-image.

1. **Life Activation.** The first was the process called Life Activation (which I mentioned earlier in the book). This activation connects the physical DNA and the spiritual DNA and finished off the last of my weight loss and the brightening of my soul. The woman in the mirror began to morph right before my eyes. This experience is powerful and dynamic. (You can go to

https://empoweredliving.academy or https://www.modernmysteryschoolint.com to read more about Life Activation and to find a certified Life Activation practitioner near you.)

2. **Empower Thyself.** The second step that transformed my self-image was the two-day class called Empower Thyself, which ended with an initiation. With the tools given to me during that weekend, I was able to know myself, grow in beauty and grace and sustain a life that is filled with light.
3. **Galactic Activation.** The Galactic Activation took me to another level of progression toward the adam kadmon body, which is also described in the glossary.

Following these three steps will help you progress through similar transformations and release your own negative story.

OUR BODY REFLECTS OUR SOUL

My current body simply reflects the state of my soul just as it did when I was a baby. I have shed some of the layers of false protection that I thought I needed as a child and young adult. What is necessary to maintain recovery from addictions and disorders has become a part of my daily routine. This body is simply a "rental vehicle" for my authentic self. Activations and initiation into the lineage of King Salomon have contributed to who I am today - an expression of divine beauty! This can be your story as well.

Today, I see the "Beauty of the Divine Expression" in everyone I meet. I look in their eyes, and I see, peering out at me, their divine selves, the selves that are beautiful and wise and healthy. I want to call forth that person to take his or her place in the world so, together, we can bring about world peace.

Remember the beautiful young man at the beginning of the chapter? With hard work and several years of intense psychotherapy, he discovered his true nature, finished college and has a rewarding career in the health field. His experience was long and arduous. Imagine how much quicker that could have happened with Kabbalah.

To embark on this journey, ask yourself the question: *What is it that I love about myself?* Always start with the positives. Then ask yourself: *On a scale of 0-10, 0 being self-contempt and 10 being loving myself completely, where am I now?* Being truthful with yourself is the first step. Then, make a decision to improve your score over the next year by asking the right questions as we discussed in Chapter Four. The following exercise will help facilitate the process to a more positive self-image.

Tools of Transformation
THE GOD OR GODDESS IN THE MIRROR

You are going to need a little hand mirror for this. Just put it beside you for now.

SETTLE IN

Find somewhere that is quiet and where you will not be disturbed.

Sit down with your back well supported, your feet on the floor and your hands in your lap in a receptive position.

Put the tip of your tongue on the roof of your mouth behind your front teeth.

BREATHE

Begin by taking a deep breath in through your nose and out through your mouth.

Do this two more times and give yourself permission to relax.

As you continue to breathe and relax, imagine that each breath in contains peace and love.

And now imagine that each breath out expels all negativity and stress.

Continue breathing in this way, taking the life force energy of your breath deep into your belly and completely expelling all negativity.

IMAGINE

Remaining relaxed, pick up your mirror and look deep into your own eyes.

Be sure to breathe.

Say out loud, "I love you," and imagine that you mean it.

Say it again and keep saying it for as long as you can without looking away.

What did you see?

What did you hear in your voice?

What did you feel, sense or know?

WRITE

Journal your experience. Draw a symbol or picture of yourself as the completely loved being that you are.

Try doing this every day for thirty days.

Notice what happens in your life.

I would love to hear about it!

Write your answers down or draw a picture in the space provided on the next 2 pages.

The key to transforming your self-image is Love.

Begin your thirty-day challenge here.

Now get ready to learn how to transform those two difficult companions - pain and suffering - into grace and wisdom.

CHAPTER 7

Moving through Pain and Suffering with Grace

Turn your wounds into wisdom.

—OPRAH WINFREY

In the book, *The Hiding Place,* Corrie ten Boom tells about an event that happened to her while confined in a concentration camp during World War II. She was being held in barracks only large enough to house a fraction of the number of women that were actually held there. The women were not only severely malnourished, but abused by the guards daily. Just when she didn't think things could get much worse, the building became infested with fleas.

In an act of faith, Corrie decided to find a reason to be grateful for the fleas instead of giving in to despair. Because of this alteration in perspective, she was able to see that the guards were leaving the building and its residents alone for the first time since she had arrived. This meant that she and the other women could freely gather together to pray and give one another encouragement. These gatherings became game changers for many of the prisoners and hope was restored in a seemingly hopeless situation.

What if every mishap in life could yield a harvest of lessons from which we could live life differently? What if the challenges were the doorways to a life filled with positivity, goodness and beauty? They are! Kabbalah facilitates the exposure and healing of the negative ego, which is the home of all dark and heavy thoughts and emotions. While being presented with the negative aspects of yourself can be unpleasant, the harvest of life's lessons is invaluable. With a little help, you can transform your own pain and suffering into wisdom and understanding.

LISTENING TO THE MESSAGES OF THE BODY

In November of 2018, I learned a powerful healing modality, called Ensofic Ray, while at a Modern Mystery School class in Toronto. The morning I was preparing to return home, I slipped on the stairs of the Airbnb I was staying in and went crashing to the bottom of the staircase, crushing my right wrist and snapping the two major bones of my forearm in half. The pain was indescribable!

So, what does that have to do with cleaning up my negative ego and Kabbalah? Kabbalistically, I asked myself why this event happened and what I could learn from it. Asking those questions helped me to realize that, at the time of the slip, I was feeling annoyed and thinking about that annoyance before I started down the stairs. The stairs were definitely slippery and treacherously constructed, and it would be easy to see how the average person could slip in this situation. But I had trained in martial arts for eight years, taught mindfulness to others and had been a regular meditator since I was nineteen years old. Navigating a dangerous staircase should have been a no-brainer for me. And, yet, I fell. My preoccupation with the annoyance, all related to the negative ego, took me out of the realm of gracefully moving through time and space and into the world of hurried mindlessness.

I asked my Higher Self what I could learn from this accident and I was shown the stark reality of the messiness of my brain and heard a resounding SLOW DOWN.

I didn't realize the full scope of this message (or what a slow learner I could be) until after I subsequently slipped on black ice in February and broke my little finger (same hand but no further damage to the wrist or arm). Shortly after that, I sprained my left ankle pretty badly.

THE VICTIM IDENTITY: PAIN VERSUS SUFFERING

You see, Kabbalah does not prevent one from experiencing pain or unexpected trauma, but it does help to clear up those things within ourselves that contribute to personal drama. There is a saying, "Pain is inevitable, but suffering is optional." The tools I learned in Kabbalah helped me to deal with the pain, and also taught me how to stop prolonging it by releasing thoughts and feelings of helplessness and hopelessness.

In the past, I nurtured a victim identity that constricted my energetic system through stress. This dampened the immune system and the body's innate orientation toward healing and wholeness. Suffering is truly optional, as I have discovered.

Kabbalah helped me to see that I am best served by keeping my mind clear of judgments, which lead to irritation, etc., and to slow down mentally, emotionally and physically. No, God didn't make me fall down the stairs to teach me a lesson! I fell, and the lesson I could learn was that I needed to create a life with more balance, built on a foundation of self-care and deep love for self.

FACING ILLNESS

Another example of the impactful way that Kabbalah has worked in my life during times of grief and pain is the effect it had on me during the time my grandson was at death's door. I mentioned this story earlier, and it is worth going into further to illustrate the power of living Kabbalah.

On August 2, 2014, my daughter, Krista, came over with four of our grandchildren. She and I were talking about the process of Life Activation, which I had just learned. She asked me if I would do that for Michael, who was eight years old at the time, as he seemed "really tired and not like himself."

They had gone to a professional soccer game the day before, and Michael had a hard time walking from the car to the field. This was very unusual for this energetic little boy who loved soccer. I turned to Michael and asked him if he wanted grandma to do something that might help him feel better, and he said yes.

I did the protocol for him and was surprised by my experience. There were a couple of things that seemed odd. After I finished the activation, I experienced a chill going through me, along with a sense of foreboding and I asked Krista to take him to the pediatrician the next morning. She had already decided to do so as a result of her own intuition.

After an examination and some tests, the pediatrician told Krista to take him to the emergency room at Mott Children's Hospital in Ann Arbor. They were there for a long time. My husband decided to go to the hospital to keep them company, and this is what he said:

> *At about midnight, a very young doctor came in to tell us of the test results. You could tell that she was very uncomfortable, but eventually she said the Big C word. I almost*

didn't catch it, probably because I didn't want to. But there it was...cancer...leukemia - and he needed to be admitted to the hospital immediately. We were shocked!

Later, we were to find out that the type of leukemia he had was typically found in adults and that the subtype was particularly difficult to treat.

GRANDMOTHERING WITH GRACE

One of the truths I had learned in Kabbalah is: **All the power that ever was or will be is here now.** I cried out to the powers that be, "Where is that power and how are we going to facilitate healing for our amazing grandson?"

It was a call to arms! Grandma and Grandpa were certain of one thing - we would not let this dear boy go without a fight. We were spiritual warriors, and the battle was on.

THE KABBALAH WAY: BALANCING THINKING AND FEELING

Several things stand out in this five-and-one-half-month sojourn.

One was my own peaceful way of being during this stressful time. In Chapter Three, I shared how, during my first Kabbalah journey, in one of the alchemical ascensions, I moved from a state of mind filled with fear and anxiety (that had been with me for most of my life) to one where my mind and emotions were balanced.

Because of this shift, I was able to be my authentic self and not let the atmosphere of a children's cancer ward and my grandson's trial overcome me. And that is really saying something, not only because of my previous emotionality, but also because I am highly sensitive and empathic, and that can be both a blessing and a curse.

BEING AN EMPATH

An empath is someone who is like an emotional sponge for the emotions and energy of the people around them, among other traits. As a child, I could not sort out the feelings that were genuinely mine from those of other people. It made life very challenging. But it also opened a door for me into how the people around me were feeling and allowed me to offer comfort where needed.

There was such a swirl of turbulent emotional energy on that ward where our grandson, Michael, was during this time!! First were the feelings of the little ones. They were experiencing things I could barely imagine. Between the chemotherapy, surgeries, radiation therapy and the sickness due to these treatments, they were confused, sad, angry, depressed and in pain.

There were also the triumphs of those little souls - the bravery, the determination, the endurance and the downright defiance of the odds. I could barely contain my joy on those transcendent days! Go little ones, go!! Show us all how to live and to love fiercely.

THE HEROES OF HEALTHCARE

And then there were the nurses, child advocates, the play therapists, music therapists, art therapists, nursing aides, the transportation staff, the housekeeping staff, all those who worked in imaging and phlebotomy, technicians and food service staff and the volunteers. These were the human angels who supported these little ones in their journey with cancer.

I can honestly say that I have rarely seen so many compassionate, loving, kind people in one place. And I was aware of their bravery and the sorrows that they swallowed in caring for their innocent patients. I was acutely aware of the personal issues that they so carefully left at the outer door of the ward so as to be present to those for whom they cared.

The staff of doctors was another storm of emotions. Confined by the matrix of the medical model, many of the doctors oozed the conflictual energy of discovering that medicine was more of an art than a science. They went into this field to heal and help. Nobody had prepared them for what they would face in their practices.

My brave and funny grandson, Michael, was a favorite of many of the staff. Although he needed to close off much of his soul to survive this ordeal, his engaging smile and indomitable nerf gun warrior spirit warmed my heart and the hearts of others around him.

And then there were the bad days. The days of constant nausea, headaches, fevers, diarrhea and vomiting and just plain old boredom. Going from a very active eight-year-old to having to be tethered to a hospital bed could sometimes just be torture.

I was aware, and I remained balanced due to the change that occurred in Kabbalah. What a miracle! I could genuinely be lovingly present to all those around me in this vast cesspool of grief and pain. That, in itself, was healing for me and those around me. And it was proof that something in me had shifted...permanently. That balance of mind and emotions that had been so elusive to me for most of my life was now a part of me. I had the ability to respond rather than react. I was finally response-able.

HEALING

After Michael's first round of chemotherapy, his blood tests did not show the presence of any cancer cells. However, the next months were difficult. The treatment that Michael was receiving was experimental and the protocol required four rounds of chemotherapy. We still had a long way to go.

Now, the challenge would be to keep him alive while these powerful but harsh drugs not only attacked the cancer, but also the rest of his body as well. I saw the toll these treatments took on his body, mind and soul.

No one should have to go through this!

The cry of my heart joined the cry of the other mothers, fathers, grandparents and loved ones of a child who was suffering. There were several points along this trail of tears that illuminated the power of Mother, Father, Creator God and the supernal triad, as shown in the Tree of Life. And I was grateful.

A few of those illuminating moments were the beautiful people who brought the Ensofic Ray (a powerful modality of healing) to Michael. One was my Guide, Barbara Segura, who would come to Detroit from Naples, Florida to administer this incredible healing to Michael while another Healer administered Ensofic Ray remotely. Each time, there were marked improvements in his bloodwork and overall well-being (see glossary).

Another significant point in Michael's journey occurred after his second round of chemotherapy. Michael was very, very sick. In fact, he was in ICU with very rapid breathing, a high temperature, vomiting and diarrhea for many days.

His grandpa, my husband, felt strongly prompted to go to Toronto for the Healer's Two Academy through the Modern Mystery School in Toronto, although it would mean leaving us when Michael was in crisis. This was a step beyond becoming certified to do Life Activations and gave him many more tools to use in this battle.

This little boy was in ICU the entire time that Grandpa Joe was gone, with no improvement. Grandpa came home, went to Michael's room and waited until Michael's father was asleep. He did healing work for several hours. He then went to a different part of the hospital and did a Spark of Life healing for Michael, and then returned to Michael's room. He continued to flow Light and *love* to him. In Joe's words:

At one point, around 4:30 a.m., I just knew I was done. I got the distinct impression to sleep, which I did. I woke up to the sound of Michael playing cards with his dad and noticed that there was a food tray with evidence that Michael had been eating! The nursing records recorded that, at the 5:30 a.m. rounds, Michael's temperature was 99.8, his respiration slowed down to 22 breaths per minute and there had been no gastric disruptions since before midnight. All I could think to myself is, "This shit works."

Michael continued to improve, and they kept him in ICU for one more night for precautionary measures. Then, they sent him back to his room on the pediatric oncology floor.

ROUND FOUR

After the fourth administration of chemotherapy, Michael was desperately ill. In my eyes, he was barely clinging to life. It was a "grandma day," and I had spent the day in ICU with him. Being relieved by my husband, I went home that night. I couldn't get the sound of his painful panting and the pale, translucent color of his skin out of my mind. It was New Year's Eve, and, with the sound of fireworks outside my window, I picked up my cell phone.

I was desperate, and, although I knew very little about technology at the time, I evidently sent a message on Facebook Messenger to Founder Gudni Gudnason. I have only God and Founder Gudni to thank that he received and responded to the message.

This conversation between Founder Gudni and me tells the story of Michael's miraculous healing. Without our involvement in Kabbalah, we may never have known of this possibility. Here are some excerpts:

1/1/2015 12:25 a.m.
ME: Please send light and life to my little grandson, Michael Grossmeyer, who is suffering with leukemia. Thank you for all you do.

1/1/2015 3:16 a.m.
FOUNDER GUDNI: So sorry to hear that, I will send light! What is being done?? And where is he located?

1/1/2015 7:23 p.m.
ME: He finished his last of 4 chemo protocols at Motts Children's Hospital, University of Michigan, Ann Arbor, Michigan. That's where he is. Barbara Segura, our Guide, has done numerous healings for Michael as well as Sue Ananian did 2 Ensofic Ray healing protocols. My husband, Joe Elwart, just finished Healer's Academy 2 and so has been doing a number of different healings for Michael including a Full Spirit activation. Our Detroit and Naples group have all been praying for him for the last six months. Any other suggestions?

1/1/2015- 7:47 p.m.
FOUNDER GUDNI: Please send me full name, address of hospital and his photo (recent one if you can.) LOVE
ME: Michael James Grossmeyer, 1540 East Hospital Drive, Ann Arbor, Michigan, U.S.A. He is on the 7th floor, room 11 facing NE.

1/1/2015 8:17 p.m.
ME: His date of birth is June 25, 2006. Both of these pictures were taken within the last 30 days. Our deepest gratitude. LOVE
ME: We just got word that he is finding it hard to breathe.
FOUNDER GUDNI: OK sending help now, hope it's not too late… LOVE
Me: Thank you. Much LOVE

1/2/2015 9:29 p.m.
ME: With my deepest gratitude, little Michael only spiked a fever 2X's today and his breathing is back to normal. He has turned the corner! Blessings and LOVE
FOUNDER GUDNI: We will continue to help, let's see if/how we can reverse this… he is not beyond help… but faith is needed.
ME: THANK YOU and LOVE

1/3/2015 7:42 p.m.
ME: Michael is 16 hours w/o a fever, no nausea. Neutrophils just showing up, still <1. CT scan showed that there "might be a fungus." Breathing is normal. Grandpa and a friend are doing "spark of life" healing once a week. Thank you, thank you, thank you. Any other suggestions? LOVE yes, FAITH!

1/4/2015 later that evening
FOUNDER GUDNI: We will do what we can for little Michael, he has a mission he needs to serve, so we will do our best! LOVE

> *1/6/2015 9 p.m.*
> ME: Michael was miraculously discharged from the hospital TODAY! Our deepest gratitude to you and I wish there were better words to express this!! I did a Snoopy dance when we got the word, kind of like your little dancing guy above.
> FOUNDER GUDNI: AWESOMENESS… soooo good… LOVE

Isn't that incredible? I was now witness to the magnificent possibilities that change lives. Through God, Founder Gudni, the teachings of the Modern Mystery School, the power of sacred Kabbalah and the prayers of many good people, my grandson was healed and, today, five years later, there is no sign of cancer.

Some of you may be facing your own challenges. In fact, I know you are. Please be assured that there is a way to change your perspective to be able to see the miraculous opportunities that are available.

CHAPTER 7

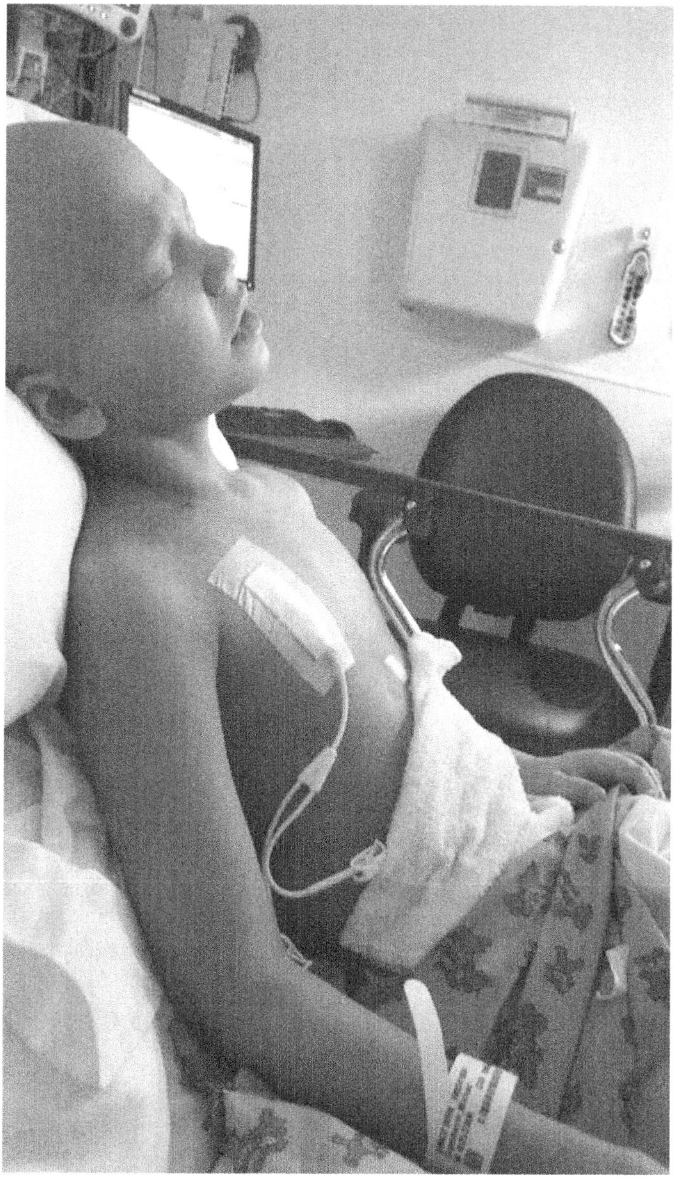

My eight-year-old grandson Michael at
Mott's Children's Hospital in Ann Arbor, Michigan.

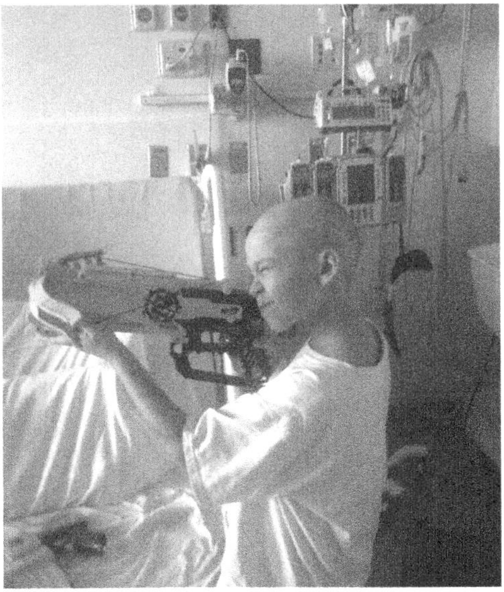

King of the Nerf gun wars.

Happy, healthy, sassy 13-year-old Michael - cancer free.

Tools of Transformation
DOORWAY TO GRACE

SETTLE IN

Sit down somewhere that is quiet and where you will not be disturbed.

Sit down with your back well supported, your feet on the floor and your hands in your lap in a receptive position.

Put the tip of your tongue on the roof of your mouth behind your front teeth.

BREATHE

Begin by taking a deep breath in through your nose and out through your mouth.

Do this two more times and give yourself permission to relax.

As you continue to breathe and relax, imagine that each breath in contains comfort and peace.

And now imagine that each breath out expels all negativity and stress.

Continue breathing in this way, taking the life force energy of your breath deep into your belly and completely expelling all negativity.

IMAGINE

Continue breathing and think of something that you find particularly challenging in your life right now.

Move that challenge into your creative mind and imagine that it is a doorway.

Just visualize the doorway.

What does it look like? What color is it?

Do you experience any sound or smell as you create this doorway?

Notice that above the door are the words 'Know Thyself'.

Imagine that this doorway is the entryway into knowledge and wisdom.

WRITE

What was your challenge?

Describe the doorway in as much detail as possible. Draw it.

What would happen if you stepped through the doorway of "knowing thyself"?

How might your challenge be transformed?

I have used this meditation on a number of occasions for different challenges that I have faced with some very unexpected results. I'd love to hear what your experience is.

The key to the doorway of moving through pain and suffering is to Know Thyself.

Step through and begin.

Divine guidance is our birthright as humans. We are part and parcel of the magnificent plan of creation. In the next chapter, we will enter into this magnificent, mystical pathway that is yours for the taking.

CHAPTER 8

The Experience of Divine Guidance

Expect the Best, Expect Divine Guidance,
Expect your Fortunes to Change, Expect a Miracle!

—WAYNE DYER

When my two older daughters were very little, we played a game that we called "Peek-a-boo with God." At dinnertime, they would announce with their excited little voices, "Mommy, God peeked at me through the clouds!" or "Mommy, God was in the butterfly!" or "Mommy, I saw God in my friend!!!" Life for them was filled with magic, and seeing the world through their innocent eyes provided us with the awareness of God in all things. Mother Teresa said, "I see God in every human being," and, honestly, so did they.

Growing up, we may become dulled to the reality of God around us, or we may lose the ability to see God at all. Our lack of awareness can cause us to lose sight of the promptings of the Divine.

Has this happened to you? Do you remember a time when magic was real, and your imagination was a tool for creation?

Kabbalah, as the path back to God, opens up a doorway to the reality of the divine by raising our recognition of the magical mysteries in every aspect of life. Connecting with this path heightens our intuitive abilities to read the road signs provided for us and remind us of our true purpose.

DIVINE PROTECTION

The presence of God in my life has evolved and broadened as time has passed. From the time I was a small child, I had a very unusual relationship with Jesus. I became aware of His presence during the years that I was being abused. He was always there, offering comfort and hope. From my childlike perspective, He, and the beings who accompanied Him (angels?), kept me alive and sane despite the things that were happening to me. I don't really know how. It was like I was living two completely different realities. It wasn't until much later in life that I questioned why He didn't stop the abuse. I just remember how grateful I was that He was there.

In addition to this, at nineteen years old, I had an instantaneous healing from my addiction to amphetamines, which, again, saved my life. "Jesus Saves" was a saying that was literal to me.

Let me be clear. This Jesus was not like the Jesus who was presented to me in church. He wasn't surrounded by man-made perceptions and assumptions. He didn't have the opinions that man had attributed to Him. He didn't even look like the pictures with which I was familiar. He was just...different.

Sometimes, He was a being of pure love, pure light, the ultimate place of acceptance and safety. And, since I was subjected to life-threatening danger on a regular basis as a child, this was a really big deal. This Jesus loved me, *really* loved me...without judgment in any way. The way He looked at me was the opposite of the "bad little girl" my abuser said I was. His love was a blanket of hope that surrounded my soul.

I tell you this in preparation for the story I share next (which I mentioned at the beginning of Chapter Two). These events were my divine guidance to stepping into my true purpose in life. It also led me to Kabbalah in strange and mysterious ways.

CONVERSATIONS WITH JESUS

One morning, at 3:30 a.m., I was awakened by a Presence that I recognized from my childhood and innumerable points in my life since then - a warm, comforting Presence. It was Jesus as I had come to know Him.

I got the distinct impression that He wanted me to come downstairs into what was then our family room for a "visit." I could feel His presence very strongly and was instantly filled with a sense of peace and joy. There was no part of me that was afraid, which, as I look back on it, was perfect. We "visited" for roughly a half hour, and then He was gone. I went back to bed and fell asleep without any problem, which was also remarkable since I had suffered with a sleep disorder for the past fifty years.

The year was 2007, and these conversations took place, periodically, over several years. The exact time is not completely clear as I only have a portion of the notes that I kept during that time. I was in my mid-fifties.

This began a journey that was mystifying, often disconcerting and always remarkable. So much of what was transmitted were topics that I didn't have a framework for in my limited experience with the metaphysical. Sometimes, what was being communicated required me to look up the words because I simply didn't understand them. These experiences were the road signs which led me to the path of spiritual progression I am on today.

I was able to share these experiences with my husband, Joe, and not only did I receive no judgment from him, but he encouraged me! I am incredibly blessed to have this courageous and loving man in my life. His support kept me from truly thinking I was crazy.

DNA

One of the themes that Jesus brought up over and over again had to do with DNA. Science is not a strong point for me, but I did the best I could to observe and absorb. It did not occur to me that what he was showing me could have been for another time. And it surely was.

Some of the writings, as I look back on them, were peppered with my own perceptions and thoughts. And some of them were clearly not because they were so far out of my paradigm at that time. A sampling of these conversations follows:

FEBRUARY 2009

Jesus: *Spend time with me daily and I will show you my way. It is the way of my DNA - that is what was made in our image and likeness.*

Me: *I don't understand Lord...*

Jesus: *The changes I want to make in you (and all people) are so fundamental that your present humanness is in your way. I want to redefine what it means to be human - my people have missed it.*

Me: *I'm lost.*

Jesus: *When I said to take dominion over the earth, I didn't mean for mankind to ruin it. With the changes mankind has wrought, your DNA has changed. You are fifty-seven, your body hurts, you are tired, your thinking is fuzzy, your eyes and ears are failing. That is not my plan. So, I need to...*

[It appears like he is taking off the top half of my head and a double helix rises up like a spiraling ladder. He touches different places with his finger, and they light up. They become a single strand. I see the neur-onet (his description), and it is lit up like a Christmas tree and very sparkly. I feel deep peace.]

"Do not be afraid," He says. And I'm not afraid, although the word 'weird' comes to mind.

DECEMBER 2008

Jesus: *Interesting, isn't it? [There is a floating, spiraling double helix between us.] He continues touching it and lighting it up.*

Me: *I want to hear about the evil that you spoke of that is moving in fast. I feel its pull on me.*

Jesus: *The purpose in you, and all of mankind, is over-shadowed by the darkness around you.*

Me: *I just want to be by your light.*

[He lifts his arms and tremendous light beams from him.]

Me: *I know you said, "Greater things than these you shall do." I feel so weak and powerless. There is so much frustration inside me.*

[I see him playing with the double helix, and then I see him with a potter's wheel with the helix floating above it. I then see myself in a dungeon's cell, saying, "Let me out! Let me out!" And the ascended Jesus comes, and it all melts away.]

Jesus: *It is the imprisonment of your mind. I am about the changing of minds.*

[I see the neuronet, and he does the same thing with it as he did with the double helix, touching parts of it.]

Me: *Do whatever needs to be done to fix this.*

Jesus: *Chris, it's not broken. It is just incomplete.*

[And then he gives me rubber boots so that I do not get electrocuted while he works.]

Other things which Jesus says that are relevant to this story:

In another visitation, Jesus said, "Do not be afraid of the Kabbalah [I had never heard of this and spelled it phonetically]. *It is indeed my way. Watch and see what it is that I want you to do.*

He also referenced "watchtowers," which I was not familiar with. It was at this time that both Joe and I noticed as time went on that each of his visitations were from 3:30 a.m. to precisely 3:59 a.m. - twenty-nine minutes.

Each of the pieces of information that Jesus shared (DNA and "lighting it up," Kabbalah and "watchtowers" and being with me for precisely twenty-nine minutes) had significance that I did not understand at the time. He was preparing me for what was next. Let's fast forward to 2012.

CLARITY & INSIGHT

In 2012, I went to visit a friend in Florida who introduced me to a friend of hers. I was somewhat reticent because this woman owned a shop called Shaman's Blessings, and my religious upbringing had me cautious of anything outside of it. (I guess the visitations by Jesus were within acceptable boundaries, in my mind, though they probably would have been judged as delusional or even arrogant.)

Arriving at her friend's house, my friend disappeared, and I somewhat nervously talked with Barbara who turned out to be a very open and friendly woman who was around my age. I felt assured when she told me about her Native American heritage and how she was raised in a convent for part of her childhood. Ah, common ground.

We chatted for a while, and I felt a kinship with her almost immediately. I asked her, at one point, what she did for a living, and she innocently said, "Well, one of the things I do is called a DNA activation." She had my *full* attention. Barbara went on to explain what a DNA activation (now called a Life Activation) was, but all I heard was: *DNA, light up, double helix*. I was catapulted back to my visits with Jesus and the things He was saying that I was trying to understand at the time!

Needless to say, I had no idea that this modality that Barbara and Jesus described was from an ancient school that was over 3,000 years old. Something in me lit up like the Fourth of July!

Barbara continued to talk and, at times, said, almost word-for-word, what Jesus had said to me. She referenced not only DNA, but also other key words and phrases. At one point, she said, "Are you all right?" She said I looked like I had seen a ghost.

I then spilled out my experiences during my visitations and noticed that she was not only very attentive, but didn't seem surprised. So many of the things she was talking about were things that Jesus had shared with me years before. Of course, I did not yet realize that these teachings and healings were from the lineage of King Salomon, which was Jesus' lineage as well.

I knew that I needed to pursue this, and I was scared to death. I suspected that the dogmatic world that I had created and lived in would either implode or explode and me along with it.

I asked her for a DNA (Life) activation right then and there, which she did. I then asked her how I could learn to do that for others. I realized that many of the messages from Jesus referenced me doing the DNA thing for other people.

Barbara told me about a class called Empower Thyself, which she said would be the next step to Healer's Academy where I would learn to do Life Activations for other people. I could barely contain myself. In my mind's eye, I looked over at Jesus, and He gave me a little grin. As I look back on it, He was the only way that I was going to be able to step off the beaten path into this world of magic and mystery. It was His guidance and assurance that kept me going.

COME WITH AN EMPTY CUP

I invited Barbara to Detroit and set up a time to have the two-day Empower Thyself class. Joe was less than thrilled. There was a part of him that was just as invested in dogma as I was. However, through the years, he had developed his own relationship with Jesus, and when he checked in with Him, he got the simple message, "Learn it." He agreed to have Barbara come.

I invited two other women to join me for the class. I did not know what to expect, and Barb encouraged me to, "come with an empty cup." Looking back on it, I did fairly well at keeping an open mind, with a healthy measure of skepticism, during the class. I struggled with some of the concepts and almost shut down at one point. However, she assured me that I did not have to believe anything I heard and that I should let the ideas incubate and apply my discernment.

We were given a number of tools, and, just when I was struggling heavily, we learned a process called *The Affirma-*

tion to Healing in which we used the word 'watchtowers', which was such an unusual word for me and one that Jesus used during our visits. I was reminded of why I was doing this. I was doing this to follow divine guidance. There were many things in this class that resonated with His visitations. I was being guided, moment by moment, along the path of liberation as the Pattern on the Trestleboard says (another tool I learned in Empower Thyself).

Yes, I was being guided. That guidance has been continual for the last eight years. I have learned how to be a healer, a teacher and a spiritual warrior. Kabbalah helped to clear the way for each of those things to happen. Do not get me wrong; life has not been without challenges. However, my life today is so far beyond anything I could imagine. I discovered that my purpose is to bring about world peace, one person at a time, activating and initiating those seekers who come onto my path. Maybe you are one of them. Wouldn't that be exciting! I would love to meet you!

This is all to encourage and inspire you to discover and define your own divine guidance! Ask yourself the question: What *guidance have I received that I might have overlooked or discounted?* Sometimes, we miss the road signs, or misinterpret them. But they are there. My path to my purpose is unique to me just as yours is unique to you. The world needs each of us to step into our divine purpose and do our part - and that includes *you*. The world is waiting!

Tools of Transformation
ACKNOWLEDGING DIVINE GUIDANCE

Along life's journey, there have been times when God was playing peek-a-boo with you. In fact, I believe that there has been a trail of heavenly breadcrumbs meant to lead you to the gates, above which it says, *Know Thyself.* This is a very important task in anyone's life. It is in coming to know ourselves that we will discover the Divine.

SETTLE IN

Sit down somewhere that is quiet and where you will not be disturbed.

Sit with your back well supported, your feet on the floor and your hands in your lap in a receptive position.

Put the tip of your tongue on the roof of your mouth.

BREATHE

Let's begin by taking a deep breath in through your nose and out through your mouth.

Do this two more times and give yourself permission to relax.

As you continue to breathe and relax, imagine that each breath in contains peace and love.

And now imagine that each breath out expels all negativity and stress.

Continue breathing in this way, taking the life force energy of your breath deep into your belly and completely expelling all negative energy.

IMAGINE

Imagine a situation in your life about which you would like guidance - perhaps a decision about your job or how to resolve a family issue. It could have to do with a legal problem or the next step in your life.

Once you settle on an issue, imagine holding a box with a question mark on it.

Place a symbol of your chosen issue in the box.

Now imagine that your Higher Power, Higher Self or the God of your understanding is in front of you. It may be a beautiful light, a person or an amazing energy, whatever depicts this best for you.

Now give the box to this divine being.

Receive the message that is coming your way. Receive the love and peace that accompanies that message.

WRITE

What issue did you settle on? Write it down as a question to be answered.

Write down and/or draw what you sensed, saw, heard or felt about your Higher Power.

Write about the feelings you had as you turned this issue over to your Higher Self or Higher Power.

Continue to journal about different messages you may receive about this issue over the next month. Be watchful and curious.

The key to Divine Guidance is your awareness.

Play with that idea now. This is the place to begin.

Divine guidance is yours for the taking. No one is excluded. Feel free to email me at christinecelwart@gmail.com and share your experience.

Well done!

What if every challenging experience is a door opening to your divine path and purpose? With the right perspective, this is not just a possibility, but a probability. Let's see how.

CHAPTER 9

Challenge or Opportunity

Nobody can hurt me without my permission.

—MAHATMA GANDHI

As a younger woman, I spent many years sitting at the tables of various Twelve Step meetings. I listened to story after story of people who had experienced life challenges only to find the doorway to a life free from the behaviors and substances that had enslaved them.

One such story was that of a young woman who was in a bar with a man who was being very abusive toward her. This was a familiar experience for her, and, as she tried to pull away from him, she drunkenly tripped and crashed into another young man who was sitting there. As he helped her to her feet, he whispered in her ear, "Let's get out of here." In a flash of clarity, she excused herself from the scene and met him in the parking lot. He drove her to her first Alcoholics Anonymous meeting, and she now has twenty-eight years of sobriety and is leading a movement that has saved the lives of countless people.

There could have been a very different ending to her story.

In Chapter Seven, I shared how I had inexplicably fallen down some stairs and severely injured my wrist. There could have been a very different ending to that story as well. With the tools of Kabbalah, I received a very unexpected opportunity. It is pretty amazing.

BROKEN WRIST CONTINUED

My youngest daughter, Renéa, who was with me, took me to the nearest emergency room. At first, it seemed like the process was quick and efficient. And then the experience took a turn for the worse.

I was told that my wrist was crushed and that I had broken both bones in my forearm completely in two. Hence, the grotesque angle of my arm when my friends lifted me from my fall.

After twelve hours, and some unfortunate circumstances, I decided to have my daughter take me to the hospital near my home for treatment.

All of my attention was captured by the pain on that ride home. I suppose that was a good thing because we found ourselves in the midst of a terrible snowstorm, which made visibility almost impossible. Our normal four-hour ride home became longer. But we got there by calling upon the heavens and the prayers of many people.

My daughter is a magnificent spiritual warrior so, there was very little drama despite the circumstances. I am so grateful to her and the many people whose prayers accompanied us on that adventure.

At the hospital near my home, they confirmed the diagnosis of a crushed wrist and broken bones. However, they told me that my bones had not been set properly and that they would have to reset them. The resetting had to be done without anesthetic and was excruciating. They sent me home and I was instructed to see a highly recommended hand and wrist specialist for further treatment.

One week later, I was scheduled to go to Florida to meet with my Kabbalah group for the second ascension experience. Instead, I had surgery to insert a plate and ten screws to keep my wrist together. There was such an opportunity for falling into PLOMming (poor little old me-ing), and, honestly, the aftermath of this surgery was one of the most painful experiences I have had as an adult. Physical pain is a particular trigger for me.

KABBALAH AND PAIN

So, how did Kabbalah change the way this experience could have gone? As I have shared before, Kabbalah is a process of learning to ask questions, the right questions, and to remain balanced. It helps one to observe, without judgment, the events of life from the perspective of the soul.

As stated earlier, I was painfully abused as a child, and one of the results of this was Post-Traumatic Stress Disorder (PTSD). When life got to a certain level of stress or pain, I would experience a PTSD episode. These episodes were peppered with extreme anxiety, panic attacks, nightmares and feeling unsafe 24/7. I would become exhausted and move into depression and want to crawl into bed with the covers over my head.

I spent many years in therapy learning tools to handle these episodes, including Meditation, Mindfulness, Eye Movement Desensitization and Reprocessing, Emotional Freedom Technique, dream work, regressive therapy, intra-psychic talk therapy, parts work, body work, and inner child work. There were many more modalities that I explored that promised some relief from the throes of these episodes.

In time, I learned to manage these occurrences, but they didn't really go away. Breaking my wrist could have led me to one of those episodes. It had all of the right ingredients to set off a post-traumatic stress experience; pain that I could not change and feelings of helplessness. These elements could lead me down the rabbit hole into hopelessness, depression and despair. But this time, intense pain did *not* lead to a PTSD episode.

THE POWER OF THE PATTERN ON THE TRESTLEBOARD

What changed my experience of pain? My experience of living Kabbalah reminded me to use one of the tools I now had: The Pattern on the Trestleboard. This is a series of powerful truths about ourselves that correspond to the different sections of the Tree of Life. Because it is so powerful and transformative, I recite it almost every day of my life.

The key to calming my survival brain during this ordeal with my wrist was to recite one statement from this Kabbalistic devotion: "The Kingdom of Spirit is embodied in my flesh." Through meditating on this, I had grown to understand the reality of this statement. I was able to access my spiritual mind and remember that I am an eternal Spirit and that this body is a rental vehicle that I will one day leave behind. This statement, and the awareness it brings, allowed me to access the Kingdom of Spirit within me and rise above the pain. Due to this expanding reality, and the incredible healing I have received through Kabbalah, I am no longer a victim to my circumstances.

This is miraculous to me! What began as a challenge turned into an opportunity for life-changing healing.

This is one of the golden opportunities you can have as a student of the Universal Kabbalah, as taught by the Modern

Mystery School. Experiencing life from a completely different perspective makes all the difference in the world.

WHAT WOULD YOU DO?

Another example of how a challenge transformed into an opportunity occurred between my first and second Kabbalah experiences.

In the fall of 2017, in my twenty-sixth year as a psychotherapist, I received a notice that a complaint had been filed against me. It concerned an adult client who had just concluded therapy with me a few months earlier. Shortly afterward, I found out that another complaint was filed by a client that I had not seen since 2011. I was shocked and dismayed. In all my years as a therapist, I had never received a complaint of any kind, and, now, there were two!

When I asked my recent client about the event, she said that she had not made the complaint and assured me that she would report to the investigator that she was happy with the services I had provided. I was confused, hurt and felt betrayed. Over the years of providing therapy for hundreds of people, I had always had positive feedback.

The complaint from the client (let us call her Mary) who I had not treated since 2011 had a particular sting to it. Mary claimed that I had engaged in "a dual relationship," which meant that we had a friendship outside of the therapeutic setting. This was true, and I completely owned that. However, one of the major events in her complaint occurred many years after she had moved out of state and was due to a desperate circumstance on her part and my response to it.

I remember the day that Mary arrived on my doorstep. It was shortly after Christmas and was icy and cold. Mary looked disheveled, upset and forlorn. After inviting her into my home, she told me her story. Mary had moved back into town and was staying with a friend. This friend had just thrown Mary and her dog out of her home. (The fact that Mary's friend had thrown her out in the middle of winter should have been a clue to the possible trouble that taking her into my home would cause me!)

She said that she was having a condo renovated, and it was completely torn apart and uninhabitable. She also explained that all her funds were held up by the contractor and that she was now homeless until the condo was finished. She was in tears. She asked if she and her elderly dog could stay with us until the condo was finished. She explained that she thought it would be a few weeks at most that she would need to stay with us. And so, we did what compassionate humans do: we took her and her dog in from the cold and offered them a place to stay.

She ended up staying with us for four months.

INVESTIGATION

And, then, years later, this woman, who had introduced me to Barbara Segura and the Modern Mystery School and whom I had taken into my home, filed a complaint. At the time, this felt unfair and unjust to me. Why was I being treated poorly by someone I had taken in at a time when she was desperate?

Before Kabbalah, I would have responded with anger and seen myself as the victim. I would not have been able to see where this situation was leading. I would have seen it as a tragedy and a betrayal. But part of living Kabbalah is to see things from the eagle's eye view. This allowed me to see what was the highest and best good for everyone.

Have you had situations like this that seemed unfair and unjust? How did you respond?

Kabbalah helped me see this difficult challenge as an extraordinary opportunity.

LETTING GO

In the last ten years of my psychotherapy practice, I had become aware of how much I was operating within an unhealthy system. I felt the mental, emotional and spiritual squeeze produced by those elements. The increasing invasiveness and control by the insurance companies continued to escalate, and I had considered retirement for several years to pursue my more spiritual endeavors. I dragged my feet because of my love for the people I was working with.

I seriously weighed the pros and cons of fighting this complaint against me. I could have been embroiled in a process that had the potential to last for the next one or two years for the ability to stay in a system I no longer believed in. The stress of these cases, by the report of others who have been through them, could be intense and exhausting.

Although it had been a gray area to take my former client into my house, I knew I had done my best for her. At the same time, I fought back the old sense of shame that once occupied my life like a ravaging wolf. I sought spiritual guidance and listened to the words of one of my teachers who also had been in the mental health field and had, himself, felt the pressure of working in the mental health system. He shared that among other things, he had become a life coach as a means of helping people in a different way.

This option was like a breath of fresh air, and the eagle within me was soaring, seeing the larger view. I agreed to not renew my license and to cease practicing as a Limited Licensed Psychologist. It was my "punishment" for having a friendship with a previous client. I received paperwork that said this in very critical terms. Although I knew I was innocent of doing harm to Mary, I was incredibly challenged to stay in the truth of who I am. This challenge presented me with another opportunity to heal the sense of shame from my past.

STEPPING INTO MY TRUE PURPOSE

What was the larger picture? What opportunity was going to come out of this?

The experience of living Kabbalah supported me in seeing this unjust situation as a blessing. This unexpected and unwelcome event became a vehicle for stepping into a fuller expression of what I had already been called into.

I am called to be a Guide, teacher, healer and spiritual warrior in the lineage of King Salomon. I am a spiritual coach and I am called to bring about world peace, one person at a time, beginning with me. I had been pursuing spiritual training for several years and now, I had the opportunity to create a life using the tools I had already received.

Six months after letting go of my practice, I found myself stepping more fully into my purpose as a Guide for the Modern Mystery School, which I do not think I could have done while so deeply entrenched in the world of psychology. Every day, I experience the energetic shifts that allow me to continue to fulfill my mission.

Today, I am not a victim of any system. Rather, I am victorious! This is what I am here for! This is verified, daily, by the fruits of my life today. I am experiencing more peace, love and joy than ever before, and my awareness of who I am and the divinity within me grows daily.

Tools of Transformation
VICTORY OVER VICTIMHOOD

SETTLE IN

Sit down somewhere that is quiet and where you will not be disturbed.

Sit down with your back well supported, your feet on the floor and your hands in your lap in a receptive position.

Put the tip of your tongue on the roof of your mouth.

BREATHE

Begin by taking a deep breath in through your nose and out through your mouth.

Do this two more times and give yourself permission to relax.

As you continue to breathe and relax, imagine that each breath in contains peace and love.

And now imagine that each breath out expels all negativity and stress.

Breathe and allow yourself to relax.

IMAGINE

Think of a time when life was unfair, or you felt victimized in some way.

Remember that part of who you are today is as a result of your history.

Now, take the incident into your heart space and imagine what it would look like if you had walked away from that incident victorious.

What would that look like?

What would you hear?

What would you feel, sense or experience?

Sit with this victory, and really feel it.

WRITE

Write about and/or draw that transformed picture.

Write down five things that you have to be grateful for as a result of this incident.

Begin to transmute the energy from victimhood to victory.

The key to opportunity is the transformation of the challenge.

Begin to create that change here.

Yes, Victory!! Remember that every change we make within ourselves is a pebble thrown into the pond of our collective experience. The ripples it produces affect the lives of those around us. Let's look at how these personal ripples can change families.

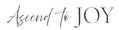

CHAPTER 10

Kabbalah, A Family Affair

The strength of a nation derives from the integrity of the home.

—CONFUCIUS

For generations, my ancestors have been very child-oriented. There is a story about my great-great-grandmother that illustrates this very well. It is said that she was a servant girl who was impregnated by a baron in Germany and gave birth to a baby girl. She was not of the noble class, and the baron demanded that she relinquish her baby to him to be raised in the castle without her.

In the middle of the night (so the story goes), she took her baby girl, my great-grandmother, and fled the country, eventually landing in the area of Ontario, Canada. I have thought of this young girl and her infant child making her 4,000-mile trek across the lands and waters without the conveniences of modern transportation and am amazed at her strength and devotion.

That ancestral strength has spurred me onward to be an example for my daughters and their children and their children's children. My goal is to model life without the limitations of history and circumstances. When my spiritual path benefits my family, it is not just a bonus; it is a sign to me that I am moving in the right direction. It shapes my discernment.

It is largely because of my children and grandchildren that I have pursued my spiritual path so fervently and haven't given up in the dark times. When I couldn't do something for myself, because of a lack of self-love, my love for my family was my motivation. This love runs deep in my blood. It is part of my DNA.

THE TREE OF TRANSFORMATION

With that in mind, let me tell you the story of how the Tree of Life, and the experience of living Kabbalah, has transformed my family.

First of all, we have four incredible daughters ranging in age from thirty-five to forty-four. We also have a spiritually adopted daughter who is actually older than we are! She has been with us for twenty-seven years and has added such an element of light into our lives. Along with our daughters, we have fifteen awesome grandchildren, ranging in ages from one to twenty-four. We are fortunate enough to be favored with two great-grandchildren, as well as two more on the way. We are excitedly waiting for the numbers to increase through the adoption of a grandson who has been with us through the foster system for three years. Talk about rich! We are blessed beyond measure by this family of amazing people.

We are all vastly different and these magnificent people have the potential to change the world. Nine of us, including our spiritual daughter and two grandsons, have been Life Activated, and eight are Initiates in the lineage of King Salomon. Five of us are Kabbalists, and all of us are on a spiritual journey. These foundational activations and initiations have given us a common bond and tools with which to share our journeys and make life richer than we ever imagined. It has also given us the means to know ourselves and to deal with life with less and less drama.

LET IT BEGIN WITH ME

The first effect of Kabbalah on the family is the difference it has made on my role within the family. As I experience continuing clarity about my true purpose and receive healings for things that have been blocking me from the fulfillment of that purpose, I have been able to be more present to my family.

I have learned to ask the right questions and catch myself when I fall into judgment or opinion. I see this reflected in the ways that we relate to each other. It has undoubtedly changed our family constellation.

PEACEFUL PARTNERSHIP

In addition to my personal development, my marriage has become increasingly peaceful and exciting all at the same time. To have a life partner who is also a Kabbalist is an enormous blessing. Life continues to present its challenges, for sure, but we approach these events so differently than we did in the past. And we have an effective means for discussing them. And let's not forget the powerful tools we have received to work through the challenges of life.

Before Kabbalah, like most couples, we had complementary triggers. This is a nice way of saying that we irritated one another on a fairly regular basis. You know that thing he does with the toothpaste that you hate and vice versa? We used to deal with it by noting the irritation, figuring out why we were irritated and concluding that it was the other person's fault - resolving nothing.

Now, being response-abled people, we take a different approach. We can own our part of the communication and change it instead of trying to change the other person. What a relief!

Of course, as has been a theme while writing the book, a perfect example of the difference Kabbalah has made in my communication with my husband occurred last night. He looked at me and asked if I was feeling irritated. After knowing each other for almost fifty years, hiding was no longer an option. I took a deep breath, and then said, "Yes, and I don't know why." This led to the Kabbalistic method of asking the right questions, and I discovered, upon reflection and with his support, first what the trigger was, and then why it was being triggered.

More Kabbalistic questions helped to illuminate and name the fear beneath the trigger. The fear had to do with what people would think of me as they read this book. It was a fear of vulnerability. Wow! I am so grateful to be able to have that in the conscious realm so that I can effectively deal with it and not sabotage the completion of this book or the peace in my home. Because that is what happens in many cases - the unconscious fears sabotage the fruition of our dreams.

So, what were the right questions in this case and how did they help?

What am I feeling? I am feeling afraid. *What exactly am I afraid of?* I am afraid of being judged.

Where did that fear come from? How old am I as I experience this fear?

I flashed to an experience that I had when I was ten years old. I was in the fourth grade and was preparing for my Confirmation. I was taught that I was going to be commissioned as a soldier of Christ, and I took that very seriously.

One afternoon, I was alone in my bedroom thinking about my Confirmation when the Jesus I knew appeared in my room. He radiated *love* and simply stood in front of me. I instantly felt reassured. And then, He was gone. I excitedly ran downstairs and told my mother that I had seen Jesus! I not only remember the shocked look on her face, but also the disapproving and sharp tone of her voice (my perception) as she said, "Don't tell anyone that!" I felt like I had done something wrong and had been slapped in the face. I had shared something very personal and sacred and felt judged.

So, in Kabbalistic fashion, once I had the awareness, I took action, forgave my mother and moved past it. With that, the irritation was gone. I was centered once again and could enjoy the rest of my evening with my husband. And I could get back to writing the book. What had been in the unconscious was now out in the open for healing and a return to myself as I really am. Mind you, all of this took, maybe, ten minutes.

Can you imagine how powerful that is in the daily interactions of a marriage? Conscious, peaceful existence is one of the keys to longevity in a marriage. Of course, having an evolving, willing partner who is also a Kabbalist really seals the deal.

Let's see what my husband, Joe, has to say about living Kabbalah. I took the opportunity to interview him about his experience of Kabbalah, and the following are his insights.

JOE'S EXPERIENCE OF KABBALAH

What has Kabbalah been like for you?

Like you, I experienced, in the ten months, transformative power for healing by going through the sephiroth or the aspects of the Tree of Life. These opened up different aspects of who I am as it does for everybody.

I had kept myself in one form of therapy or another for years and years. I adhered to the belief that, in being a therapist myself, I couldn't guide anyone else to anyplace to which I had not gone. I kept working on myself until the effort was more than the benefit. Then, I would move on.

With the backdrop of those many years of therapy, and hearing people talk about the amazing ways that Kabbalah cleaned up the negative ego, I thought: Oh, this will be interesting to see what fragments are left. And, boy, was I surprised. There were big pieces in there! Pieces that I had worked on for years came bubbling up, and I was able to deal with them on whole new levels.

Everything from insecurities to anger to frustrations and inertia. I found myself at times just not wanting to do anything and pushing through that. Every area of life that I thought I had dealt with came up and showed some aspect of difficulty within me. I realized just how fragile my stability was and how much more work could be done.

Kabbalah cleaned me out in ways and to degrees that was far deeper, far faster and far more thorough than any of the therapeutic modalities that I had previously experienced.

Kabbalah consistently brought about healing, strength, growth and confidence with peacefulness.

How do you think Kabbalah has affected our marriage?

Only for the better. We have had some incredibly wonderful times and some horribly hellish times. I think it took us from a good place and brought us into a far better place.

An example of this would be how neither one of us follows the triggers that we used to follow. If something comes up, each one of us, separately, deals with our own triggering stuff and brings ourselves back to a place of centeredness without relying on what the other person does or doesn't do, says or doesn't say. I am responsible for my piece, and you are responsible for yours. It has dramatically improved the quality and depth of the good parts of our relationship and continues to hone away and eliminate any unpleasant aspects.

So, how do you see the experience of Kabbalah affecting our overall family?

The effect is incredible. The confidence that each of our girls has after taking Kabbalah, the peacefulness, the centeredness, the focus has all changed. There are so many skills and tools that each of us use now in dealing with our own lives and in communicating with each other. It's stuff that was there to begin with, but it has been cleaned up, polished and is running so much easier, so much smoother. Our life as a family flows. There is this flow, and we support each other. We are there for each other, and, at the same time, each one of us takes full responsibility for our own lives. We are simply sharing what is going on and what is beyond each one's current ability to shape what each is dealing with whether that be the legal system, the mental health system, the foster system, the physical health system or the weather.

When anyone is facing situations, whether of life-changing magnitude or everyday challenges and victories, we share it. We respectfully support and share experiences and pitch in to help where help is wanted. I have seen miracles happen as each one of us uses the various gifts and tools that we have learned through the Mystery School and Kabbalah.

I have also watched as these extraordinary results not only benefit our family, but society at large.

Any closing thoughts?

Yes. The five questions (Who am I? What am I? Where did I come from? Where am I going? and What is my purpose?) that we journaled about every day in Kabbalah resulted in a deep, profound knowing of who I am, what I am, where I came from, where I am going and what my purpose is. In other words, the meaning of life became clear and, if that is not a significant enough reason for someone to take Kabbalah, there isn't going to be anything that will move somebody to do this.

If you have a spirit, a soul, a hunger for life, taking Kabbalah can only make things better.

Let this be encouragement to all of you who are reading this who are married or partnered. This shared spiritual path, not based on dogma or the opinions of mankind, can be so life-giving to a relationship. You have an opportunity to relate, from your individual truth, to each other in a deeper way.

In my sixty-eight years of life, I have learned that there are very few absolutes in life. I discovered that instead of the black and white with which I had painted life, there is, actually, a rainbow of colors and variations that is expansive and beautiful. This is my experience of living Kabbalah: gloriously colorful with the ability to give a family a multi-hued foundation with which to transform not only the individual members, but its very structure.

Joe and me today. Partners as we ascend to joy.

Tools of Transformation
FAMILY, TRIBE, COMMUNITY

SETTLE IN

Sit down somewhere that is quiet and where you will not be disturbed.

Sit down with your back well supported, your feet on the floor and your hands in your lap in a receptive position.

Put the tip of your tongue on the roof of your mouth.

BREATHE

Begin by taking a deep breath in through your nose and out through your mouth.

Do this two more times and give yourself permission to relax.

As you continue to breathe and relax, decide that each breath in contains hope and healing.

And now decide that each breath out expels all negativity and stress.

Continue breathing in this way, taking the life force energy of your breath deep into your belly and completely expelling all negativity.

IMAGINE

Take a few moments to relax.

Whether it be your family of origin or your family of choice, imagine that everyone in your tribe is supportive and loving toward one another. If you do not identify with a group in this manner, then take this time to imagine what your group would look like.

Either way, see them celebrating together with harmony and respect.

Take a few minutes to create this picture.

See the happy, relaxed expressions on their faces and the healthy glow of their interactions.

Stay here for a while with yourself at the center, contributing to this feeling of well-being.

WRITE

Who and what did you see? Draw your chosen community.

What did you hear, taste, smell and touch?

What can you do this week to create this sense of community?

Write the results of your experiment.

You are amazing!

You are the beginning of Shamballa, peace on earth and good will toward mankind.

Remember this.

The key to peace on earth begins with the family.

Peace in the family begins with you. Have fun!

The pursuit of living Kabbalah is challenging and gratifying. Let's look at more of the fruits on the Tree of Life.

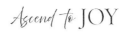

CHAPTER 11

The Fruits of Kabbalah

But the fruit of the Spirit is love, joy, peace, patience, kindness, goodness, faithfulness, gentleness, and self-control.

—GALATIANS 5:22-26

About twenty years ago, a young couple came into my office looking bedraggled and war-torn. He had an angry scowl on his face, and she looked like she had not slept in weeks. They sat on the loveseat without touching, and the air was filled with tension. She said, "At the lowest time of my life, he has started drinking again." He replied with, "I've done everything I can. She hasn't let me touch her in months and can barely look at me." They had lost a child through miscarriage, and then he lost his job. Their marriage was in crisis and they were looking for help. Through psychotherapy, and hard work, they recovered from the train wreck their lives had become. The Kabbalah train was not yet in my toolbox to offer them, and it was touch and go for the first year of our work together.

Many families today struggle to maintain unity. The divorce rate in the U.S. continues to climb, and chronic illnesses of all kinds are on the rise. Finances, infidelity, lack of productive communication and poor coping skills have all contributed to the overall stress that relationships experience today. Add to that the lack of accessible support and the unrest in our nation, and the chances for relational longevity become slimmer.

You may have experienced some of these situations in your own life. Imagine if you had a system of relating that met each person you love right where they are, a methodology for asking the right questions and the ability to honor the divine within each person. Wouldn't that be useful and exciting? Well, that is what living Kabbalah and the Tree of Life provide!

My family has been through some difficult circumstances. We have weathered addictions, job losses, divorce, PTSD from the war in Iraq, cancer, depression, panic disorders, miscarriages, infertility, foster care challenges, legal issues and much more. Kabbalah has been instrumental in helping my family navigate these challenges as a community.

Our spiritual connection has served to give us common ground, but, at times, our connections were stretched to a point of breaking. Because we live in different areas and continue to grow spiritually, we have developed ever more effective means of communication. Kabbalah has helped with this, and, today, we keep in touch through a family chat site.

Our four birth daughters have adult lives of varying shapes and sizes. They range in age from thirty-six to forty-four. They are very different from one another, and yet they support each other in some pretty amazing ways. But this was not always true. Kabbalah has changed my daughters, as individuals, in wonderful ways. I interviewed the three who experienced Kabbalah, and their stories demonstrate the power of this beautiful tool in my family and the possibilities for all families and for you! Let me share some of the fruits that have grown on our family tree as a result of Kabbalah.

KRISTA

I asked my oldest daughter, Krista, how she thought Kabbalah affected our family dynamics, and she had many insightful things to say. She is truly a beacon of light in this world. She has birthed six of our grandchildren, taken on four more with her partner and returns to a place of joy more often than not. She is a chemist by background and is presently creating a company that will train and monitor the safety measures in chemical labs. Like everyone, though, she had her moments of stress, and she learned my flair for emotional drama. Kabbalah helped to provide her with more balance in her life.

Krista reminded me of a very difficult conversation that she and I had a number of years ago (you know those conversations that can be deal-breakers in a family). I honestly didn't know how we were going to make our way through it at the time, and neither did she. She recalled:

You said that the only reason you were able to hear me was because of Kabbalah, and I know that the only reason I was able to articulate myself the way that I did was because of the healing I received through Kabbalah.

Wow! I agree 100%. Recognizing and utilizing new ways of communicating is a huge part of living Kabbalah!! What blew me away was the next thing she said:

During the course of Universal Kabbalah, we are supposed to set a goal with intention, and I found that I just couldn't do it. And it occurred to me, during one of the classes that that, in itself, was my issue - my inability to pick a direction or trust my instincts. So, I set total healing for myself and my family as my goal.

What struck me about this was that for the past three years, our family has been on a painful and, sometimes, exhilarating path of healing at breakneck speed. We have been through so many major, but necessary, shifts for healing, and it has not been easy. I wondered, at times, why this accelerated healing was happening. Krista entered the Kabbalah journey three years ago! Now I know who, and what, was partially responsible - Krista and her desire for healing in our family and setting her Tangible, Measurable Results in that direction.

Krista continued saying:

I am not sure all this healing would have happened without Kabbalah. At first, I said it (the goal of total healing for myself and my family) flippantly, but, as I continued to work through it, I began to see the depths and magnitude of that intention. And I basically said I don't care what it takes - I do not have to live bound up in fear. I made a commitment that I was absolutely not going to live in fear. In order for that to happen, there would have to be total healing, and I accepted that it would be a very long process and I accepted that, in assuming it would be a very long process, I was already putting in some of my own shit.

And then I said, "OK, I will just keep going." I describe it like this: Kabbalah is ten years of therapy in ten months. Kabbalah has given me tools to reconnect my energetic self with my physical self, which started with the Life Activation. But, then, Kabbalah was kind of the handbook on how to interact with that reconnection. As Barbara (our Guide) said during Empower Thyself, "It helped me to remember the things I didn't know I forgot." That is one of my favorite quotes. It also reaffirmed that I have everything I need; I just have to remember how to access it.

Krista said so many other beautifully profound things in our conversation. She shared how she realized, during

Kabbalah, that, although she would love to jump ahead in her metaphysical studies, that her focus, right now, needs to be her family. She wants to pursue her studies more fully once she has done what is best for her children. Kabbalah continues to operate in her life with daily realizations and discoveries about herself and how she can minister to her family more effectively. How cool is that?

RENÉA

Renéa is my beautiful, strong, loving, youngest daughter. The thing I am most aware of in her is her amazing courage and tenacity. Before she was Life Activated and initiated into the lineage of King Salomon, she was a mess. When she was six years old, we watched the light go out in our bright and beautiful little girl. We could not figure out what had happened, but spent the next fourteen years taking her to doctors, psychiatrists, counselors, priests, healers and doing anything that we thought would help. My husband and I had resigned ourselves to making our mission to keep her alive until she found her way.

She got into many dark things, including drug and alcohol abuse. She eventually created a sober and drug-free life, but one without light and filled with rage, which does not bode well for sustainable freedom from addiction.

I invited her to an Empower Thyself class with Barbara Segura, and everything changed. During that class, I watched as my ADHD daughter, who could not pay attention or sit still, looked at Barbara with intense attention and stillness with tears streaming down her face. After her initiation, I asked her what had happened. This is what she said:

Mom, it is like I woke up and I could see color again!

I knew without a doubt that I had witnessed a miracle.

This was the beginning of a new life for my strong and powerful daughter. Since that time, she has healed her marriage, taken on the role of stepmother and grandmother extraordinaire, risen to new heights in her job and become a healer, teacher and spiritual warrior. She also served as the focal point for our family's major ancestral healing, which was facilitated by Founder Gudni and Ipsissimus Hideto of the Modern Mystery School. It is our family's inheritance from us and has changed the course of our family's history both in the past and moving into the future.

Now, let's move to this past year, five years forward, to what Renéa said in her interview:

The whole reason that I went to Kabbalah was because of stagnation. I was tired of the lack of movement in my life, and, since finishing Kabbalah, there has been a lot of movement in my life. Literally, being able to exercise regularly. Exercising is a huge change, but I also have movement in my finances. During Kabbalah, I came up with a plan to get myself out of debt. I have implemented it, and I am working toward my goal successfully.

I also noticed that, previously, as a family, we never really talked to each other, although we had the family chat. Now, we are talking to each other.

My anger is gone. Right after Kabbalah, it went away. At my final ascension, I finally got inside my body. The feeling is not as strong now as it was during my final ascension, but I am more present now. I am more in the moment now than before Kabbalah.

Kabbalah can help people in their spiritual progression in that it helps you to Know Thyself. I think that is the number one thing that is missing in most forms of spirituality, to really, really know yourself. Empower Thyself is the beginning of getting to know yourself, but it is only two days. Kabbalah is ten months, and you actually have to schedule time out of your day to do the exercises, journaling, meditations and homework. This, along with the energy shifts, helps you to truly know yourself. That makes all the difference in the world.

Basically, I would recommend Kabbalah to anyone who is stuck in their lives. I was stuck for a very, very long time, and, now, there is actually movement in my life.

My daughter's life is a miracle. And it continues to unfold in so many wonderful ways. Kabbalah has allowed me to watch miracles, both large and small, in my family. Miracles brought about by the free will choices of the individuals and the power of the Tree of Life. Let's take a peek into another experience of Kabbalah in my family.

JENNA

Jenna is my amazing second daughter and is a beautiful, smart, dynamic young woman. She loves fiercely and is funny and dedicated to making this world a better place. She has her doctorate in psychology and runs a counseling clinic that specializes in counseling children, although she sees all kinds of people.

When I asked her about her experience during Kabbalah, she said the following:

During my time in the Kabbalah class, I opened up my private practice, which was a really big deal. I was in a pretty toxic environment in another clinic. I knew I needed to get out, but I didn't know how. As we went up the Tree, there were various energies that we were working in which allowed me to take the next step, and then another, and by the time we had ascended to the supernals, I had found my office, left the toxic environment, opened my practice and had a very steady flow of clients. I accomplished, in less than ten months, what I had been thinking about for years.

Kabbalah provided me with confidence that I didn't have before, a structure to follow that I even use with my clients now: You have an Idea (inspiration), then you create with a thought, with a plan, with action and follow it through.

As far as differences in the family, there is a spiritual awareness that is coming forth in our family. There has been healthier communication in the family where people show up as their authentic selves, and my relationship with Krista has dramatically improved. I have witnessed Renéa's transformation, which has given me a lot of ease in life as I am no longer worried about her.

We have this family chat, and we all engage in it and stay connected so much more than before. If you think about it, the change in communication style, and the fact that we are authentically relating, has permeated everything else in the family structure. We have fun together, and it is the fun that comes from authentically relating. We started on a path of healing, as individuals, and there has been this trickle effect. So many of my family relationships are more real and loving.

I have to admit that I was not the perfect student in Kabbalah. I didn't read all the things I could have read or do all the journaling I could have done, and I still got so much from it. I experienced all the energies of each sephira, and some of them were very uncomfortable. The discomfort of Geburah led me to the discovery of an imbalance in myself between the pillars of mercy and severity. I was way over on the healer side of the Tree, and I needed to discover the warrior within me to balance it out. I really believe that having my warrior awakened has allowed me to do what I am doing in the foster system right now. I wasn't even aware that I had this badass warrior goddess inside of me!

Kabbalah has real-life applications, and people need to know that. In the process of Kabbalah, I accessed the courage to start my own practice and leave the security of having someone else be in charge. You can make some drastic changes in your life even when they are scary.

So many people have dreams of what they would like to do with their lives. I have yet to meet the person who cannot answer the question, "If there were no obstacles, what would you like to do with your life?" Everyone has something to say in response to that. But so many people do not believe that they can do it. People are taught to live a very limited existence. I have always known that there is so much more to this physical existence, but Kabbalah gave the name to it, gave the energies for it and taught me how everything works together, independently and interdependently. Kabbalah gave me the confidence that I can do what I have always dreamed of doing - that I don't need to live this human life limiting myself.

Listening to her made my heart sing! My wish for all of my daughters is that they become all they were created to be. My heart is full as I share their experiences because that is exactly what is happening. Thank you, daughters, for your courage and willingness to grow and share your stories. Thank you, Kabbalah.

These stories from my family show the power that Kabbalah can have not only in individual lives, but also how that power can be multiplied when our partners and family members join us in living Kabbalah. Be the change in your family system, and, whether or not they join you, your lives will all be changed. That is the power of this ancient, energetic system.

Oh, and the couple at the beginning of the chapter? I recently ran into the wife at a restaurant where they were celebrating their twenty-fifth anniversary with their six children. What a joy to see the fruits of their Tree of Life!

Tools of Transformation
FRUIT OF THE TREE

SETTLE IN

Sit down somewhere that is quiet and where you will not be disturbed.

Sit with your back well supported, your feet on the floor and your hands in your lap in a receptive position.

Put the tip of your tongue on the roof of your mouth behind your front teeth.

BREATHE

Begin by taking a deep breath in through your nose and out through your mouth.

Do this two more times and give yourself permission to relax.

As you continue to breathe and relax, imagine that each breath in contains the frequency of faith.

And now imagine that each breath out expels all doubt and disbelief.

Continue breathing in this way, taking the life force energy of your breath deep into your belly and completely expelling all negativity.

Take a few moments to relax and breathe.

IMAGINE

Imagine your life as a tree with the branches representing all the different facets of your life.

Now, imagine that on that tree are various fruits representing virtues, qualities or relationships that you want in your life.

Imagine each of these as a different fruit hanging from the tree.

Change anything you want in this picture until you feel a sense of satisfaction.

Take your time. Prune anything that is not satisfying to you.

WRITE

One last time, take out your pen and write in this book or your journal.

What does your tree look like?

What do you hear? Taste or smell? Draw your tree.

What do you feel when you look at the fruit on your tree?

Write about what you would change in your life and pick one thing to begin changing now.

The key to a fruitful tree is your imagination, openness and courage.

Begin to apply those here.

CHAPTER 11

The fruits of Kabbalah have been rich and satisfying for my family and me. Personal peace, love and joy, as well as family love and support, are the exquisite fruits that we are growing. Join us and call upon your inner master gardener to cultivate not only an exquisite tree, but an orchard filled with good fruit!

CHAPTER 12

The End of the Beginning

Now this is not the end. It is not even the beginning of the end. But it is, perhaps, the end of the beginning.

—WINSTON CHURCHILL

This is my story of Living Kabbalah, for now. I wrote this knowing that you, too, can transform your life and live in joy. There is a roadmap that is embedded in your DNA that will lead you to God within, and God without, and, because it is there, the road just keeps leading to new joyful adventures.

Here is an example of the continuing power of Kabbalah. I just finished the second ascension of my third Kabbalah class. Preceding this ascension experience, I had a photoshoot for this book, which was very outside my comfort zone. Why? Because my self-image is still evolving. However, I know, without a doubt, that I am being guided to a more joyful view of myself as evidenced by the following story.

As my photographer was working, he would show me different shots that he had taken. My breath was taken away. In these photos, I saw a beautiful, wise woman who radiated light, *love* and joy. I flashed back to the 'woman in the corner' story from Chapter Six. I realized that through living Kabbalah, I *am* that woman in the corner. I saw in these photos the SAME woman Jesus had shown me thirty years ago. I am even wearing white in the photos, just like my vision of that woman. With a startling awareness, I realized that who I am today is how God has always seen me. Thank you, Kabbalah, for that new lens through which to view myself!!

The Woman in the Corner.

What if you could see yourself through the eyes of the God of your understanding? What if you believed that you were an eternal being and, as such, had never been born and would never die? What if you could see every other human with the eyes of God? How would life be different? If you are anything like me, it would be joyfully life-changing. This is the power of living Kabbalah. I can't wait for the next chapter of my life because this is only the beginning.

Can you feel it yet? I know some of you can. Living Kabbalah takes you up the staircase of your DNA, to your Divine Nature Always. It answers the important questions in life. It breaks through the glass ceiling of your limiting beliefs and manifests in Tangible, Measurable Results, to the life of your dreams.

Whether you are looking for healing for yourself and your relationships or responding to a hunger in your soul, or just curious, you owe it to yourself to explore this path of progression, evolution and *JOY*.

TAKE THE NEXT STEPS

What I have shared in this book, and hopefully you have experienced in reading, meditating and writing, is just a drop of the living Kabbalah experience. At this point, you may be intrigued, or at least interested in, how to access the power of Kabbalah in your life more fully and deeply. Here's how:

Do you want to . . .

1. Dip your toe in the water?
2. Splash around for a bit?
3. Jump ALL IN?

DIPPING YOUR TOE

Dipping your toe into the water is getting a Life Activation. A Life Activation is a process that is life-altering for many people. The procedure takes about an hour and is administered by a Certified Life Activation Practitioner with the Modern Mystery School (both my husband and I are certified LAPs). You can go to https://www.modernmysteryschoolint.com and look for a Life Activation Practitioner in your area or email me at christinecelwart@gmail.com and I'll make sure you connect with a Certified Practitioner. Give yourself the gift of a Life Activation and experience life connected to your Higher Self and to your purpose.

What does that look like? Well, here are some of the benefits that have been experienced by those receiving a Life Activation:

- Recharges and revitalizes your physical body
- Clears out negative thoughts and emotions
- Amplifies your connection to your Higher self and spirit guides
- Increases your intuition and spiritual gifts
- Shifts your consciousness to make positive changes in your life
- Allows you to use more of your brain power
- Lights up your auric field
- Brings clarity to your life

Receiving a Life Activation is a necessary piece before you enter a Universal Kabbalah program of study with the Modern Mystery School. And, even if you go no further, this alone will change your life.

SPLASHING AROUND

Bless yourself with an Empower Thyself class and initiation. There are two levels of learning that happen here. First is learning about the many mysteries that have been hidden for 3,000 years since King Salomon gathered information from around the world. Secondly, you receive tools and energetic keys to improve your life on a continual basis. I use these on a daily basis at least twice a day. Empower Thyself is also required before you begin Kabbalah. Some of the benefits of taking Empower Thyself, listed on the Modern Mystery School website, that I can personally attest to are:

- The empowerment of 10 times more Light energy to direct toward your goals, dreams and desires in life
- Receive ancient tools and sacred rituals that initiates have used for thousands of years to awaken their divinity and align themselves with their true purpose
- Greater awareness and connectivity to your own intuition and inner guidance
- Access to hidden secrets of the mysteries of the universe
- Unlock the answers within yourself to questions such as, Who am I? Why am I here?

- Capability to grow your chi and protect your own personal energy field
- Permission to work with Angels and Light beings in a deeper way
- Permanently align your personal will power to flow in alignment with the will of God, Nature and the Universe
- Create a foundation of positive Light energy for you to more easily handle the challenges and obstacles that come up in life
- Ability to access further training in the Modern Mystery School, including higher initiations and deeper mystery teachings

As I have shared, the energetic tools provided through this class not only change lives, but also, in some cases, like with my youngest daughter, saves lives.

Again, there are two ways to access an Empower Thyself class. One is to look at our website, Academy for Empowered Living, https://empoweredliving.academy, to see when the next Empower Thyself class and initiation are offered in the Detroit area. We would love to meet you! Or contact https://www.modernmysteryschoolint.com for a class that is in your area. With these you will have given yourself unimaginable tools to make your life magical.

JUMP ALL IN

After the Empower Thyself class and initiation, a next step on the path is to take Universal Kabbalah. Each class is ten-to-twelve-months long and includes monthly study groups, either in person, Skype, Zoom or on the phone. In addition to this, there are four alchemical ascension days or weekends that you will attend in person with your group. Most groups are twenty to forty people, and, even though they may be spread throughout the globe, you will get to know them in warm and wonderful ways.

Check the Modern Mystery School calendar at https://www.modernmysteryschoolint.com to see where and when the next class is taking place.

Tools of Transformation
CHOOSE ONE, OR CHOOSE ALL OF THEM!

1. Receive a Life Activation.
2. Take an Empower Thyself class and receive an initiation.
3. Sign up for a ten-to-twelve-month Universal Kabbalah class through the Modern Mystery School.

To receive a Life Activation or take Empower Thyself contact me at christinecelwart@gmail.com, or look on our schedule at https://empoweredliving.academy.

To take Universal Kabbalah or find a practitioner in your area of the world, visit the Modern Mystery School at https://www.modernmysteryschoolint.com.

Come live Kabbalah and guide yourself to a more joyful life. It is a blast!

And in closing, I leave you with these words of wisdom:

When you reach the end of what you should know,
you will be at the beginning of what you should sense.

—KAHLIL GIBRAN

What lies behind us and what lies before us are small matters compared to what lies within us. And when we bring what is within us out into the world, miracles happen.

—HENRY STANLEY HASKINS

Acknowledgements

There are so many people who had a part in this book, and I am beyond thankful for their inspiration, perspiration and support along the way. My soul-felt gratitude goes to: my heaven-sent editor, Heather Davis Desrocher, who is a fellow Kabbalist and dear friend; my amazing new friend, April O'Leary, a publisher of light; my awesome Kabbalah teachers: Founder Gudni Gudnason, Verla Wade, Teresa Bullard, Eric Thompson and Barbara Segura, who is my Guide, sister and Kabbalah leader; and my fellow Kabbalists in the Modern Mystery School.

My heart is also filled with thanks for my daughters and courageous Kabbalists, Krista, Jenna and Renéa, for their willingness to share their stories. And, of course, my daughters, Elena and Shirana, who although not Kabbalists yet, have been two of my biggest fans. A huge debt of gratitude goes to Joe, my husband and lover of forty-six years, my best friend and my greatest support. I am so honored to be your wife. You are a magnificent spiritual warrior who continually encouraged my visitations, inspirations and messages from the divine. *And* you continue learning to discern and grow on this adventure, all with a huge grin and the ability to break out into spontaneous song at any moment! I truly look forward to what the next forty years will bring.

Founder Gudni Gudnason, how can I thank you for bringing Universal Kabbalah to the Modern Mystery School? You continue to change so many lives. You have not only provided me and my family with the tools of transformation, but you have also provided them to the world as well.

And, I am so grateful to you, dear reader, for responding to your inner guidance by reading this book because the seeds of change in this world lie within you. We always have a choice. Your choice to broaden your horizons and tap into the hidden mysteries of the universe is awesome. There is so much more to learn and to experience.

Glossary

ASCENSION - Heightening of one's consciousness to a higher level. We ascend into a higher dimension of understanding, and we have access to much more knowledge as we ascend higher. The ascension process that we experience in this Kabbalah is through the Tree of Life. As we ascend up the Tree, learning about the Tree and its different aspects, we expand and grow in the understanding of life and life's mysteries.

BABY BLESSING - This is a specialized process that is administered by a Certified Practitioner at the time of a baby's birth. This procedure can be done at a later time, under certain circumstances. It is part of the lineage of King Salomon and provides the child with a brighter, more energetic future.

For more information, contact Joe Elwart, who is certified to do this blessing at https://empoweredliving.academy or christinecelwart@gmail.com, *or contact* https://www.modernmysteryschoolint.com *for other practitioners.*

EMPOWER THYSELF - This course will introduce you to metaphysical concepts and ancient teachings to *empower* your life with the secrets of the sages that have been kept hidden throughout history. You will learn about how your own energy system works, how the hierarchy of light and heaven is structured, how to work with the archangels and angels to guide your life, as well as sacred tools such as rituals, meditations and prayer. This is a two-day program, and its completion is marked with a sacred initiation ceremony.

ENSOFIC RAY - Administered by a highly trained practitioner, the Ensofic Ray is the highest, brightest and most powerful ray of energy. It has the qualities of purity, clarity and focused concentration. This healing modality is a process of re-orienting body, soul, and spirit to each other for absolute alignment: first, by destroying imbalanced physical, mental and emotional patterns that prevent our highest potential; second, by sealing our physical vessels (our bodies) to contain this highest vibration; and, third, by harmonizing our structures (mental, emotional and physical) so that we can create a full life without conflict.

For more information, contact me at
https://epoweredliving.academy or to find a practitioner
near you, contact https://www.modernmysteryschoolint.com

GALACTIC ACTIVATION - Following the Life Activation, there are two codons that are not activated. They are called the Galactic Code (physical DNA) and the Divinity Code (spiritual DNA). All mystery school traditions have taught that, when humankind is ready, they would receive a technique to activate the last two codons. The activation of these codons would result in what is called the *adam kadmon* or the god-human. The Galactic Activation is this process.

For more information, please go to https://www.modernmysteryschoolint.com

INITIATION - Serves to ground the spiritual energies you are wielding, such as light, power and protection. To 'initiate' means to begin a process, to start something. Initiation sets forces in motion for your own personal metamorphosis and spiritual journey. All your own experiences and knowledge of your journey to this point are only enhanced with the knowledge, keys and energy received at the Empower Thyself program and initiation.

KABBALIST - In this book, this term is used to describe people who have gone through the Universal Kabbalah process.

LIFE ACTIVATION - This is the twenty-two-strand DNA activation that awakens your divine blueprint and heightens your connection with your Higher Self! While enabling you to bring in and hold more light (positive energy) in your physical body, it also empowers you to maximize your potential to bring forth hidden talents and abilities and gives you more energy and clarity. It begins a process of releasing unconscious patterns (old emotional traps we fall into), while increasing your ability to use more of your brain and clears family and genetic karmic patterns.

MODERN MYSTERY SCHOOL (MMS) - One of the seven ancient mystery schools on earth, it is the only one that is open to the public (opened in 1997). The western headquarters is located in Toronto, Canada, and there are centers in over fifty-five countries around the world. The Modern Mystery School teaches classes on ancient metaphysics that have been handed down in a direct lineage for thousands of years. MMS believes that all humans can be empowered to live in peace, joy, fulfillment, abundance and in harmony with all, while living in accordance with their own unique purpose. MMS believes that life is meant to be lived, and realizing one's own true potential is part of thriving as a spiritual and physical being.

Through the power of activation, initiation and the wisdom of the lineage of King Salomon, the Modern Mystery School provides the tools, teachings, healings, services, classes and programs that enable the initiate to transform themselves, coming into a state of truly knowing themselves.

NEGATIVE EGO - The part of the human psyche that contains all the unhealthy programming, wounding experiences and vices. Anything that is not part of our authentic, divine self.

SHAMBALLA - Heaven on earth, a place or state where mankind lives in peace.

SPARK OF LIFE - The truest form of remote energy work available to humans today. This method is very powerful as the energy travels within the inner spark of pure light from God. Go to https://empoweredliving.academy for more information.

TMR - Tangible, Measurable Results

TREE OF LIFE - An image and an energetic system used in various mystical traditions. The Tree of Life lives within each of us and is the map back to God.

UNIVERSAL KABBALAH - A pure system of inner discovery and practical experience that utilizes all aspects of the Kabbalah without being tied to any particular religious affiliation or orthodox dogmas.

About the Author

Christine Elwart, M.A., practiced holistic psychotherapy for 26 years working with people from all walks of life. She left the profession to pursue her present role as a spiritual guide to help individuals discover the meaning of their lives. She lives in Royal Oak, MI with her husband Joe of 46 years.

To find out more visit her online at
www.empoweredliving.academy.

To contact Christine, email christinecelwart@gmail.com.
She would love to hear from you!

Made in the USA
Monee, IL
02 June 2020

32375569R00115